Published by
EN Productions
P.O. Box 1653, Franklin, TN 37065
Office Phone: 615-599-5552
Office Fax: 615-599-5554
For orders call: 1-877-200-1604
www.encountersnetwork.com

GET eSchool and Other Materials

The following study guide, *The Healing Anointing,* is great for individual study in your own home, with a small group, or in a classroom setting. It also serves as part of the core curriculum for a course by the same title in our God Encounters Training – eSchool of the Heart (visit www.GETeSchool.com for more info). At the end of each detailed lesson are simple questions for your reflection and review. In a back section of this study guide, you will find the answers to these questions to aid in your learning.

If you have benefited from this study guide, James W. Goll has many other study guides and materials available for purchase. You may place orders for materials from Encounters Network's Resource Center on our website at www.encountersnetwork.com or by calling 1-877-200-1604. You may also mail your orders to P.O. Box 470470, Tulsa, OK, 74147-0470. For more information, visit our website or send an e-mail to info@encountersnetwork.com.

Dedication and Acknowledgement

Over the years, I have had the honor of knowing and walking with many anointed leaders from diverse backgrounds within the body of Christ. In the "Healing Movement Today" there are a new generation of leaders and believers who flow freely in the gifts and authority of the Holy Spirit. But it has not always been that way. There tends to be forerunners who go before the masses with a breaker anointing on their lives and open the way for others to emerge.

With this thought in mind, I want to honor and acknowledge one of my dear friends and early mentors in life, Mahesh Chavda. It was the healing ministry of Jesus flowing through Mahesh those many years ago that enabled Michal Ann and I to go from barrenness to fruitfulness. But the grace of God we brought forth children when it was medically impossible for us to have children. I will always be grateful to the Lord for the life and ministry of this dear man of God. With this in mind, I wish to dedicate this study guide, *The Healing Anointing*, to Mahesh Chavda.

Every study guide or book I do has never been a solo job. It always takes a team of people and sometimes a group over a period of years. This study guide has been through many edits, revisions, cover designs and layout formats over the years. Mercy! It is impossible for me to list out all the people who have contributed hours of labor, both paid and unpaid, to bring this project of love into your hands today.

So I will simply have to say thanks to all the present and former staff members of **Encounters Network,** formerly known as **Ministry to the Nations**. A thank you also goes to all those who have never carried a staff position, but have labored with me to bring this manual to the place of excellence that it is today.

Thank you each and every one!

With Gratitude,

Dr. James W. Goll

Table of Contents

Preface: Flowing in the Anointing

In our quest to be effective tools in our Master's hands there are many keys to learn along the way. Surely being devoted to the spiritual disciplines of meditation of scripture, studying the word of God, a life and prayer and fasting, and the encouragement that comes from being a committed member of the body of Christ in a practical way are some of these necessary tools to have in our tool chest. But there is another that is often over looked.

Honor is a key to moving in the sweetness and power of God. Yes, I said honor. We are to honor God and live as though Jesus were our divine escort. Honor our families while keeping our authority lines clean. But there is another aspect to this key of honoring. You want to honor the Lord and welcome Him in your midst at all times. Yes, honor the Lord.

To move in the anointing, you must love the anointing. To flow in the anointing, you must love the presence of God. This takes a tender sensitive heart to the very breath of God Himself. Yes, honor, love and cherish the anointing of God's presence! Oh how I love to flow in the river of God's presence. There is nothing else like it in this life. Therefore, if you want to flow in the anointing then learn to give room to Him, move over and let Him have the main seat. Let the Lord be the main attraction!

This study guide, *The Healing Anointing*, comes from learning in the trenches. This manual is more than just a bunch of techniques that will work. It has been put together to help you to do the works of Jesus Christ! Contained in this instruction book are lessons and keys to flowing in the anointing of God. I encourage you as you approach this subject, look deep – not just surface level. Hunger for the things of God and before long you won't just be sitting on them there hands – you will be laying them on people and seeing God show up!

Once again, the study guide is divided in sections. The first section is simply called **The Healing Ministry**. In it we take a look at "The Healing Ministry of Jesus" and various means that God uses to heal today. "The Five Stage Healing Model" is taught and we round up this first section with material on "Using the Word of Knowledge in Healing."

The second section is called **Releasing God's Healing Power**. We take a moment to review subjects such as the healing of rejection and emotional bondages as well as tried and true lessons on how to transform the mind by putting on the helmet of hope.

The last section is aptly titled **The Anointing**. Here we touch the needed subjects of "Compassion," "Understanding the Anointing," "Cooperating with the Anointing" and finally, "Moving with the Anointing". Valuable insights are offered that often take years to learn!

When Jesus walked into the synagogue in Nazareth on that Sabbath Day and stood up and read from the scroll of Isaiah, it was a major demarcation. History was both being stated and made. Jesus declared, *"The Spirit of the Lord is upon Me. Because He anointed Me to preach the gospel to the poor. He has sent Me to proclaim release to the captives, and recovery of sight t the blind, to set free those who are downtrodden, to proclaim the favorable year of the Lord."* He closed the book, and gave it back to the attendant, and sat down. He then released a earth shattering statement: *"Today this Scripture has been fulfilled in your hearing."*

I would have loved to have been there right at that time. What controversy must have been stirred up! Yet it was true. This Messiah that Isaiah and the many other prophets had been declaring for hundreds of years would come, was now standing in their midst. Truly, He was (and always will be) the Son of God. But notice the type of ministry that He walked in.

A ministry of salvation for the whole man was and is the ministry of Jesus our glorious Lord! When we speak of the word "salvation", we often think of the greatness of forgiveness of our sins. Oh how wonderful that is for only He can forgive sins! Yet He was saying so much more than that! The Greek word for salvation that is used here – *sozo* – brings to us a meaning of salvation for the whole person. The meaning of this simple word includes: healing, deliverance, cleansing, and anything else that pertains to life and godliness! Jesus has come to set the captives free!

But, how? He gave us the key right at the very beginning of the prophecy He quoted. *"The Spirit of the Lord is upon Me because He has anointed Me."* Is this a key for us as well that we might also do the works of Jesus? Of course it is! It is not by might nor by power but by the Spirit of the living Lord that miracles take place. Don't you want to move in the healing anointing? Then I have good news for you! You can because Jesus who lives inside of you is the same yesterday, today and forever!

When the Spirit of the Lord is upon me – I can do all things through Christ who strengthens me! Yes, you can move in the healing grace of God. Did you catch that last word I used? GRACE. Yes, it is all by grace – because, once again, this is not about us – it is all about Him!

May the Spirit of the Lord come upon you and may you be equipped to minister God's salvation to a hurt and disabled world! May the healing anointing come forth stronger in this generation than any before – all for the glory of His great name!

As usual, you will find Reflection Questions at the end of each lesson and the corresponding answers in the back of the manual. May you learn to flow in the anointing and see through your life and your hands that Jesus Christ is the same yesterday, today and praise God tomorrow! Go flow!

Blessings to You!

James W. Goll

Section One:

The Healing Ministry

Lesson One:
The Healing Ministry of Jesus

I. CHURCH HISTORY

Throughout history we have seen men and women who have carried an anointing to release the healing power of God and see lives set free from the sickness. Through the first hundred years of the Church – known as the apostolic era, healing was a common activity. Irenaeus (125–202 AD) writes – "For some do certainly and truly drive out devils, so that those who have been cleansed from evil spirits frequently both believe in Christ and join themselves to the Church. Others have foreknowledge of things to come; they see visions, and utter prophetic expressions. Others still heal the sick by laying their hands upon them and they are made whole".

In recent years we have seen those gifted of God to heal the sick in extraordinary ways such as Kathryn Kuhlman, Oral Roberts, T. L. Osborn, Francis MacNutt, John Wimber, Benny Hinn and Mahesh Chavda and many others.

II. THE WORK OF ATONEMENT

One question that is debated among theologians – Is healing in the Atonement? (Atonement means: To make reconciliation, to appease, to expiate, or make propitiation.) Was the work of Christ on the cross sufficient, not only to take our sin but also take our diseases or sickness? Here are some views to ponder.

A. A. J. Gordon (1836–1895) – Baptist Minister and Author

In the Atonement of Christ there seems to be a foundation laid for faith in bodily healing... that we have Christ set before us as the sickness bearer as well as the sin bearer of His people.... The yoke of His cross by which He lifted up our iniquities took hold also of our diseases... Christ endured vicariously our diseases as well as our iniquities.[1]

B. A. B. Simpson (1843–1919) – Founder of Christian and Missionary Alliance Movement

In Isaiah 53:4-5 – the very mirror image of the coming Redeemer... is surely the promise of healing, the very strongest possible statement of complete redemption from pain and sickness by His life and death... Therefore as He hath borne our sins, Jesus Christ has also borne away, and carried off our sicknesses; yea and even our pains, so that abiding in Him, we may be fully delivered from both sickness and pain. Thus by His stripes we are healed.[2]

C. F. F. Bosworth – Healing Evangelist
The greatest barrier to the faith of many seeking bodily healing in our day is the uncertainty in their minds as to it being the will of God to heal all. Nearly everyone knows that God does heal some, but there is much in modern theology that keeps the people from knowing what the Bible teaches – that healing is provided for all. It is impossible to claim by faith a blessing which we are not sure God offers where the will of God is known.[3]

D. T. L. Osborn – Healing Evangelist
Isaiah said of ...Christ who was to come: He was wounded for our transgressions, He was bruised for our iniquities (there's the sin question); by whose stripes we are healed (there's the sickness question), thus showing again that provision has been made for deliverance from both sin and sickness.[4]

E. Hugh Jeter – Assemblies of God Minister
If Christ bore the penalty for my sins, then I do not have to bear it. If Christ bore my sicknesses, then I do not have to suffer it. His sacrifice is complete, nothing lacking. The atonement for our sins was effected on the cross. With His stripes we are healed. Healing for our bodies, as well as healing for our souls was provided by our Lord through His atoning death. It is now up to us to accept the finished work of Christ and appropriate by faith the forgiveness or healing that we need.[5]

F. John Wimber (1932 –1997) – Founder of the Vineyard Movement
Healing is not in the atonement in the same way salvation is. However God does wish to heal and my proposal is that there are times of ebb and flow within the context of kingdom activity and this may answer the question why all are not healed at a given time as well as help us to understand why many are not healed on other occasions.[6]

Questions to ponder:
1. Why wasn't Timothy healed when great miracles were happening in Ephesus? Why did Paul tell Timothy to take a little wine to help his stomach?
2. What about Epaphroditus and Trophimus illness. Why weren't they healed?

III. VARIOUS APPROACHES TO HEALING

A. Third Wave Perspective – A Current Day Approach[7]

This approach to healing is based on the holistic model (Hebraic Worldview); that every category of healing is interrelated to other levels of healing because of the basis unity of man's nature.

1. Healing of the Spirit (Spiritual Sickness is Mainly Caused by Sin)
    Healing of the spirit is renewal and restoration of your spiritual life your relationship with God. Sickness of the spirit is caused by an individual's sin. The deepest kind of healing is the forgiveness if sins which Christ provides in response to repentance. Receiving His salvation results in the process of healing our spirit.

2. Healing of Relationships (The Social Aspect of Man)
    The violation of godly precepts results in broken relationships. Therefore the healing of relationships comes with an exchange of forgiveness and a reapplication of the precepts. Harmonious interpersonal relationships contribute to the health of the whole community.

3. Healing of Past Hurts (Memories and Emotions)
    This area of healing deals mainly with our emotional life. Things from the past in terms of bad memories, or the effects of past sins are included in this type of healing.

    While sickness of the spirit is caused by what we do, sickness of the emotions is generally caused by what is done to us. It grows out of the hurts that are done to us by another person or some experience we have been exposed to in the past. These hurts affect us in the present in the form of bad memories, and weak or wounded emotions. This, in turn leads to various forms of sins, depression, a sense of worthlessness and inferiority, unreasoning fears and anxieties, psychosomatic illnesses etc. Healing of the past hurts touches the emotions, the memories, and the person's inherited family spiritual problems.

    Remember Jesus came to bind up the broken-hearted to set the prisoners free to release the oppressed. Jesus come to free us from the evil which burdens us today, take the memories of our past and heal us along with the wounds that have resulted from them and which affect our lives in the present.

Inner healing is the discipline of the digging deep, under the guidance of the Holy Spirit, to discover whatever roots might be springing back to life, and to bring them to effective death on the cross.[8]

a)   Peter's denial of Jesus (Matt. 26:33-35; 69-75).
b)   Joseph and his adverse experiences with his brothers (Gen. 37:19-28; 39:1-23; 43:6; 45:1-8).

4.   Healing of the Body (Organic and Functional Problems)
Sickness of the body has its root in physical factors, either organic or functional disorders. Therefore, healing of the body means changing and restoring the physical conditions so that the body functions properly. Consider blind Bartimaeus (Matt. 20:20-34).

5.   Healing of the Demonized (Often Seen as Psychic or Mental Illness)
Sickness caused by the influence of demons can have the same symptoms as spiritual emotional and physical.

Therefore healing this type of sickness means the expulsion of the demonic influence and the restoration of all affected areas. An example of this is the Syrophoenician women's daughter (Matt. 15: 22-28; Mark 7: 24-30).

6.   Healing of the Dying (Comforting and Strengthening the Dying)
The idea to is bring people through the experience of death both the one dying and those who are bereaved.

a)   Centurion's servant – Matt. 8: 5-13.
b)   Nobleman's son – John 4:46-45.

7.   Healing to the Dead (Raising the Dead)
It is raising the dead a back to life. It is the visible act of God's power that clearly shows His ability to invade Satan's stronghold and overpower him on his turf. A good example is the raising of Lazarus (John 11:1-57).

B.   Greek Words for Healing

1.   Wholeness is the root word *iaomai*, one of the five New Testament Greek verbs translated as 'heal'. This word is used physically twenty-five times (Matt. 15:28), figuratively of spiritual healing five times (Matt. 13:15, James 5:16).

2. *Soso* is used sixteen times by Jesus. Taken from an Aramaic term, it has a two-fold meaning of 'to make alive' or 'to make healthy'.

3. In Mark 3:4 the word *Psuchen sozai* is used and implies spiritual as well as physical salvation. John Wilkerson writes... *Sozo's* wide application in the Gospels indicates...that healing and salvation overlap... Healing of the body is never completely separable. Healing of the body is never purely physical and the salvation of the soul is never purely spiritual, but both are combined in the total deliverance of the whole man.

4. *Therapeuo* is the most frequently used and indicates that divine healing is immediate and complete restoration to health... (in need of) no more attention.

5. *Apokathistemi* means to restore to former condition of health.

C. Hebrew Words for Healing[9]

1. *rapa, rp.* – means to restore, fix, repair, mend, remit, make whole and to heal (Ex. 15:26). The same root is used for the healing, making whole or restoring of the body and spirit, land and water, city and nation. Every instance it is used in the Bible, *rp* has reference to restoring a wrong, sick, broken, or deficient condition to its original and proper state. The Lord as "rope" could be supplicated to make infertile wombs fruitful, mend earthquake torn lands, make poisonous waters wholesome or restore an apostate people. There was great fluidity in this OT usage.

   sp. – means to gather or remove. It is found four times in the context of healing all with reference to Naaman the "leper" (II Kings 5:3, 6, 7, 11). Hence Naaman was regathered to his people from his leprosy.

2. *('lh)' ruka (cf. te ala).* – means healing of a wound or restoration. It is used three times in Jeremiah 8:22; 30:17; 33:6, always with '*lh*' and contextually coupled with *rp*' and once in Isaiah 58:8 as a prophetic metaphor. It is used figuratively for the rebuilding of Jerusalem walls (Neh. 4:1), and the repairing of the temple in II Chr. 24:13. It occurs twice in Jeremiah related to the concept of healing new skin.

3. *ghh.* – means to free (from sickness), cure. Occurs once verbally in prophetic, metaphorical usage (Hos. 5:13) and once nominally in Prov. 17:22 – *A cheerful heart is good medicine.*

4. *hbs.* – means to bind or "to tie on, up" as in "to saddle (a donkey)" (Gen. 22:3; Ex. 29:9). It is used primarily in prophetic or metaphoric usage meaning to bind up, bandage a wound (Isa. 1:6; Hos. 6:1) to bind a fracture (Ezek. 30 21; 34:4, 16; Isa. 30:26) and more generally "to bind up, heal" (Job 5:18), even to the broken hearted who figuratively speaking also need to be bound up (Isa. 61:1; Psa. 147:3).

5. *hyh.* – Just as sickness is associated with death, so healing is associated with life, and life and death, healing and life are in God's hands. Deut. 32:29 – *I put to death and bring to life (wa hayyeh), I wound and I will heal.* *Hyh* can mean to make alive or bring back to life, to live or be healed (with reference to healing the seriously ill, as opposed to resurrection of the dead) and is practically synonymous with curing diseases. Either the sick person is in danger of death - hence, being kept alive means being healed; or the sick person, because of his or her affliction, is not truly [living] – hence, to live, in the fullest sense of the word, one must be restored from his illness (Num. 21; 14: 38; II Kings 2; Isa. 38:1, Isa. 38:9, 21; Gen. 20:7; Psa. 143:11; 33:19; 41:3; 30:4).

6. *hlm* – In the sense of to become healthy, strong (Job 39:4; Isa. 38:16).

7. *metom* – means soundness. Occurs three times in the context of health (Psa. 38:4, 7; Isa. 1:6).

8. *swb.* – means to turn back. In the domain of physical healing , it means to restore (return, turn back to the previous state of health as in II Kings 5:14 – *and his flesh was restored and become clean like that of a young boy.* (I Kings 13:4-6). When used with *nepes*, *swb* can mean to refresh, reinvigorate, keep alive (Ruth 4:15; Psa. 19:8; Prov. 25:13; Lam. 1:11, 19), or simply to bring one back, rescue (Job 33:30).

9. slm.– meaning a sense of wholeness, well-being. The New Testament translates *shalom* in I Sam. 25:6 with good health (Isa. 57:18-19, Jer. 6:14).

IV. OVERVIEW OF THE HEALING MINISTRY OF JESUS[10]

Description	Matthew	Mark	Luke	John	Code
Man with an unclean spirit		1:23-25	4:33-35		AB
Peters mother in-law	8:14-15	1:30-31	4:38-39		BCD
Multitudes	8:16-17	1:32-34	4:40-41		ABCE
Many demons		1:39			AF
Leper	8:2-4	1:40-42	5:12-13		BCGH
Man with withered hand	12:9-13	3:1-5	6:6-10		BG
Multitudes	12:15-16	3:10-11			A
Gerasenes demoniac	8:28-32	5:1-13	8:26-33		AB
Jairus' daughter	9:18-25	5:22-43	8:41-56		BCE
Woman with issue of blood	9:20-22	5:25-34	8:43-48		GI
A few sick people	13:58	6:5-6			C
Multitudes	14:34-36	6:55-56			EI
Syrophoenician's daughter	15:22-28	7:24-30			ABE
Deaf and dumb man		7:32-35			BCD
Child with evil spirit	17:14-18	9:14-27	9:38-43		ABCE
Blind Bartimaeus	20:30-34	10:46-52	18:35-43		BCGH
Centurions servant	8:5-13		7:2-10		DE
Two blind men	9:27-30				BCG
Dumb demoniac	9:32-33				A
Blind and dumb demoniac	12:22		11:14		A
Multitudes	4:23		6:17-19		FJ
Multitudes	9:35				FJ
Multitudes	11:4-5		7:21		FJ
Multitudes	14:14		9:11	6:2	H
Great multitudes	15:30				FJ
Great multitudes	19:2				
Blind and lame in temple	21:14				
Widows son			7:11-15		BH
Mary Magdalene and others			8:2		A
Crippled women			13:10-13		BC
Man with dropsy			14:1-4		C
Ten lepers			17:11-19		BFG
Servants ear			22:49-51		B
Multitudes			5:15		
Various persons			13:32		A
Nobleman's son				4:46-53	BE
Invalid				5:2-9	BG

Description	Matthew	Mark	Luke	John	Code
Man born blind				9:1-7	BC
Lazarus				11:1-44	B

A. Drove out demons
B. Word spoken
C. Touched by Jesus
D. Prayer of another
E. Faith of another

F. Preaching of Jesus
G. The person's faith
H. Jesus moved with compassion
I. Person touches Jesus
J. Teaching of Jesus

V.   SUMMARY OF DEDUCTIONS AND VIEWS

A.   Holistic Model

1.   Healing is holistic, therefore we should not neglect the natural and human means to healing in our effort to minister supernaturally.

2.   Often physical illnesses are caused by emotional, spiritual or even demonic elements. The complex interrelationships between the various types of sickness, the parts of the human make up and different kinds of healing, must be taken into account.

3.   We must minister like Jesus, for we have been commissioned to heal (Matt. 10:1-8; 28:18-20). In relationship with the Holy Spirit we must see what the Father is doing and do it.

4.   Because Jesus came as a man and demonstrated that one could heal, we should follow in His steps.

5.   In the New Testament Jesus always combined healing with the proclaiming of the kingdom of God – Matt. 12:28.

6.   By healing the sick, Jesus defeated Satan and demonstrated His rule.

7.   In the New Testament healing is seen as an extension and effect of sin and is therefore evil in origin representing the kingdom of Satan.

8.   Divine healing is more than physical or spiritual wholeness; it touches every aspect of the human life that can come under the power or influence of Satan.

9. Divine Healing means:

    a) Forgiveness of Sins
    b) Restoration from sickness
    c) Breaking the hold of poverty and oppressive social structures
    d) Deliverances from demonic power and influence
    e) Raising the dead

10. Healing are signs of the presence and power of God's Kingdom (Luke 7:22-23).

11. Healing is associated with repentance from sin and conflict with Satan.

    a) Health is frequently determined by individual righteousness or sin – Mark 2:1-2; John 5:1-11; James 5:14-16.
    b) Cooperate disobedience and sin open to weakness, sickness and death – Acts 5:1-11; I Cor. 11:27-32.

B. It's All about Jesus!

Hebrews 13:8 states – Jesus Christ is the same yesterday and today and forever. The bottom line is that healing comes as a result of the completed work of the cross of Jesus Christ! What He did yesterday, He will do today and in the future. Why? God has not changed!

Let us believe and see in our day the following verse activated. Acts 10:38 – You know of Jesus of Nazareth, how God anointed Him with the Holy Spirit and with power and how He went about doing good and healing all who were oppressed by the devil; for God was with Him. So let us continue in our study together and see the fullness of the Healing Ministry of Jesus be restored in our day!

Reflection Questions
Lesson One: The Healing Ministry of Jesus

Answers to these questions can be found in the back of the study guide.

Fill in the Blank

1. Define the word "Atonement"? _____

_____

2. Define the Greek word *Sozo:* _____

3. The deepest kind of healing is forgiveness, which Christ provides in response to our _____.

Multiple Choice.– Choose the best answer from the list below:

A.	Signs	C.	Power
B.	Satan	D.	Gifts

4. Healings are _____ of the presence and power of God's Kingdom.

5. Healing is associated with repentance from sin and conflict with _____.

True or False

6. Health is frequently determined by individual and corporate righteousness. _____

7. Corporate disobedience and sin open the door to weakness, sickness and death. _____

8. Healing and proclamation of the gospel were always combined in the New Testament. _____

Scripture Memorization

9. Write out and memorize Romans 3:25; Hebrews 2:17.

Continued on the next page.

10. What was the primary point you learned from this lesson?

Lesson Two:
Healing Delivery Systems

I. GOD'S VARIOUS MEANS

A. Removing Blockades

God wants us to be well!! But, God has more than one assembly line available to Him by which He delivers the finished product. Obviously, conditions must be met in order to receive from the Lord. Knowledge of the Father's love, faith in the completed work of the cross of Christ, and patient abiding in the Word of God are but a few of these essentials.

In some situations, we try to "box God in" on how He will heal us. God has various means to utilize, to restore, or to bring us to proper health. Ignorance, unbelief, prejudices, and presumptive thinking are blockades that must be removed for the stream of God's healing power to flow to and through us.

II Kings 5:1-14 tells us of the preconceived ideas Naaman, the leprous and valiant warrior, had concerning "how God through the prophet would heal him." Verse 11 states, *But Naaman was furious and went away and said, "Behold, I thought, He will surely come out to me, and stand and call on the name of the Lord his God, and wave his hand over the place, and cure the leper."* The directions given by Elisha were to the contrary though. *"Go and wash in the Jordan seven times, and your flesh shall be restored to you and you shall be clean."*

Due to Naaman's preconceived ideas and his prideful and prejudiced ways of thinking, he almost missed out on the very thing he was seeking – cleansing, healing, and restoration. Naaman turned away in rage (v.12) but his faithful servants prevailed upon him to go and wash himself in the Jordan River. As Naaman humbled himself and did the little act of foolish obedience, his flesh was restored like the flesh of a little child and he was made clean (II Kings 5:14).

Let us also drop our prejudiced, prideful ways of thinking, humble ourselves, and receive as a little child!

B. Three Channels of Healing Love

The highest form, other than the climactic resurrection of the dead and receiving our "glorified bodies," is Divine Health.

III John 2 states, *Beloved, I pray that in all respects you may prosper and be in good health, just as your soul prospers. Good health is the mark we all desire.*

In God's healing delivery system, there are at least three major channels:

1. The natural.
2. Science and the medical arts.
3. Divine, supernatural healing.

Each of these areas is valuable and much dissertation can be done to expound on each of these separately. But, the focus of this teaching is to highlight the variety of means God uses in the divine, supernatural approach.

II. PRIMARY VERSES ON HEALING

The following are some of the classic scripture verses on healing that one should study, learn and meditate upon.

A. Exodus 15:26

If you will give earnest heed to the voice of the Lord your God, and do what is right in His sight, and give ear to His commandments, and keep all His statutes, I will put none of the diseases on you which I have put upon the Egyptians; for I, the Lord, AM YOUR HEALER.

B. Psalms 103:1-5

Bless the Lord, O my soul; and all that is within me, bless His holy Name. Bless the Lord, O my soul, and forget none of His benefits; Who pardons all your iniquities; Who heals all your diseases; Who redeems your life from the pit; Who crowns you with loving-kindness and compassion; Who satisfies your years with good things, so that your youth is renewed like the eagle.

C. Isaiah 53:5

But He was pierced through for our transgressions, He was crushed for our iniquities; the chastening for our wellbeing fell upon Him, and by His scourging we are healed.

D.   Peter 2:24

And He Himself bore our sins in His body on the cross, that we might die to sin and live to righteousness; for by His wounds you were healed.

E.   Matthew 8:16-17

And when evening had come, they brought Him to many who were demon-possessed; and He cast out the spirits with a word, and healed all who were ill, in order that what was spoken through Isaiah the prophet might be fulfilled, saying, "He Himself took our infirmities, and carried away our diseases.

F.   Mark 16:16-17

And these signs will accompany those who have believed: in My Name they will cast out demons, they shall speak in new tongues; they will pick up serpents, and if they drink any deadly poison, it shall not harm them; they shall lay hands on the sick, and they shall recover.

G.   I Corinthians 12:9

And to another, the gifts of healing by the one Spirit.

H.   James 5:14-15

Is anyone among you sick? Let him call for the elders of the church, and let them pray over him, anointing him with oil in the Name of the Lord; and the prayer offered in faith will restore the one who is sick, and the Lord will raise him up, and if he has committed sins, they will be forgiven him.

III.   BIBLICAL METHODOLOGIES

A.   Communion – The Lord's Supper

Read: I Cor. 11:27-34

God has, to a larger degree, bound our physical well-being to our ability to relate spiritually to the "flesh and bone" aspect of Christ.

For more on this subject refer to the lesson "The Blood That Speaks" in the study guide *War in the Heavenlies.*

B.   Water Baptism

Read: Rom. 6:3-6; Mark 16:16.

Perhaps some believers have never experienced freedom in habit patterns of sin because they've never identified with the death, burial, and resurrection of Christ through a New Testament water baptism. This is not an option and is commandment of scripture that should be fulfilled.

C.   Calling for the Elders and Anointing with Oil
Read: James 5:14, 15; Mark 6:13.
Be prepared to act on God's Word! Be ready to obey God's Word and anoint with oil the sick acting in faith as you release the Holy Spirit's anointing.

D.   Laying on of Hands and Prayer by Believers in General
Read: Mark 16:16-18; Matt. 19:19.
All believers have as their prerogative to believe God's Word and pray for the sick through the laying on of hands. God is looking for hands to use. Can the Lord work through your hands?

E.   By the Spoken Word
Read: Luke 7:1-10.
The greatest faith, according to Jesus, rests solely in the "Word."
There were three types of people who came to Jesus for healing:

1.   Those who came for personal healing.
2.   Those who brought someone else for healing.
3.   Those who came for someone else, but only sought the word of Jesus, stating they would be healed.

F.   Jesus' Garments; Peter's Shadow
Mark 6:56 – *And wherever he went – into villages, towns or countryside - they placed the sick in the marketplaces. They begged him to let them touch even the edge of his cloak, and all who touched him were healed.*

Acts 5:15, 16 – *As a result, people brought the sick into the streets and laid them on beds and mats so that at least Peter's shadow might fall on some of them as he passed by. Crowds gathered also from the towns around Jerusalem, bringing their sick and those tormented by evil spirits, and all of them were healed.*

These formed a "point of contact" for the one in need. The Lord will use such "tools" with us as we are led by the present tense voice of the Holy Spirit.

G.   Handkerchiefs and Aprons from Paul
Acts 19:11-12 – *God did extraordinary miracles through Paul, so that even handkerchiefs and aprons that had touched him were taken to the sick, and their illnesses were cured and the evil spirits left them.*
Notice that these were called "special/extraordinary miracles." They were done this way either by revelation or because there was no other way for Paul to contact them.

H. Levels of the Operation

There are various levels of operations such as the Gifts of Healing and Working of Miracles. See the study guide on *Releasing Spiritual Gifts* for more on this subject.

1. Instantaneous – Matt. 8:3; Mark 1:31.
2. Gradual – John 4:52; Mark 8:22-25.

I. Confession

James 5:16 – *Therefore confess your sins to each other and pray for each other so that you may be healed. The prayer of a righteous man is powerful and effective. Confess your faults to another and experience cleansing and healing. This opens a gate of humility and thus God's grace appears on the scene.*

J. Healing Release through Angelic Activity

John 5:12-17 – *So they asked him, "Who is this fellow who told you to pick it up and walk?" The man who was healed had no idea who it was, for Jesus had slipped away into the crowd that was there. Later Jesus found him at the temple and said to him, "See, you are well again. Stop sinning or something worse may happen to you." The man went away and told the Jews that it was Jesus who had made him well. So, because Jesus was doing these things on the Sabbath, the Jews persecuted him. Jesus said to them, "My Father is always at his work to this very day, and I, too, am working* (NIV). For more on this subject, see the lessons on the "Ministry and Function of Angels" in the study guide *Understanding Supernatural Encounters*.

IV. HEALING STYLES

A. Soaking Prayer Approach

Mark 8:22-26 – *They came to Bethsaida, and some people brought a blind man and begged Jesus to touch him. He took the blind man by the hand and led him outside the village. When he had spit on the man's eyes and put his hands on him, Jesus asked, "Do you see anything?" He looked up and said, "I see people; they look like trees walking around." Once more Jesus put his hands on the man's eyes. Then his eyes were opened, his sight was restored, and he saw everything clearly. Jesus sent him home, saying, "Don't go into the village."*

Bringing the presence of God into an individual's life over an extended period of time and seeing progressive healing occur through the patient process often termed "soaking prayer".

B. Five Stage Healing Model
An integrated approach to healing, which involves dialogue-prayer combination as, taught in the book, *Power Healing*, by John Wimber. This Five Stage technique is presented in full in Lesson Three of this study guide.

C. Faith Healing
1. By the faith of healer – the one ministering.
2. By the faith of individual – coming with the need.
3. By the faith by others who bring the one in need.
4. By exercising faith in the Word of God expressed through prayer to God alone.

D. Acting Out Specific Directions
This might be by putting fingers in ears, placing mud in the eye, or telling someone to dip in the pool as Jesus did. In this manner we wait to get specific direction and then "Listen and obey".

E. "Slain in the Spirit"
Resting in the Spirit, overcome by power, the "glory fall", etc. Many different terms have historically been used to describe this overwhelming experience. This experience is when one is gently or powerfully "falls in the Spirit" into a resting position where God's presence and healing moves upon your being.

F. "Lengthening of Legs and Arms"
There are numerous and various healing techniques that may be utilized and which may authentically release the power of God to flow into an individual. This may include simply sitting a person in a chair and asking the Lord to give a Holy Spirit chiropractic adjustment, as He adjusts and repositions or heals the leg or arm.

V. BEING OPEN – NOT CLOSED – A GREAT KEY

A. We Must Learn to be Faithful
Be faithful in the little we presently receive – stepping out in faith that a greater increase of His anointing will come (Luke 16:10-12).

B. We Must Drop Our Prejudices
We must drop our prejudices against particular streams, styles, and techniques. Let's not strain at a gnat and swallow a religious camel!

C. Let's Always be Christ-Centered

Let's always be Christ-centered giving praise and honor to the glorious Lord Jesus Christ, and lift up the One who suffered on our behalf. Remember the lesson of Num. 21:6-9. Whoever looked at the bronze serpent upon the standard lived. Let us lift up Christ and cause people to look to Him!

Remember, ultimately, it is not the "healing techniques or models of delivery systems" that bring God's cure to bear. It is the person and presence of the Jesus as says Matthew 4:23 – And Jesus was going about all the cities and the villages, teaching in the synagogues and proclaiming the gospel of the Kingdom, and healing every kind of disease and every kind of sickness.

Reflection Questions
Lesson Two: Healing Delivery Systems

Answers to these questions can be found in the back of the study guide.

Fill in the Blank

1. There are some 10 biblical methods mentioned in this lesson. List these ten methods.

   1. _____ 2. _____
   3. _____ 4. _____
   5. _____ 6. _____
   7. _____ 8. _____
   9. _____ 10. _____

2. In God's healing delivery system, there are at least three major channels. What are these? 1. _____
   2. _____ 3. _____

Multiple Choice – Choose the best answer from the list below:

A.	Healing	C.	Jesus Christ
B.	Gold	D	.Miracles

3. Naaman's prideful and prejudiced ways of thinking almost missed him out on the very thing he was seeking which was _____.

4. Remember, ultimately, it is not the "healing techniques or models of delivery systems" that bring God's cure to bear, but _____.

True or False

5. The highest form, other than the climactic resurrection of the dead and receiving our "glorified bodies," is Divine Health. _____

6. There are various levels of operations such as the Gifts of Healing and Working of Miracles. _____

7. Confess your faults to another and you will experience cleansing. _____

Continued on the next page.

Scripture Memorization

8. Write out and memorize Exodus 15:26; I Peter 2:24.

9. What was the primary point you learned from this lesson?

Lesson Three:
Five Stage Healing Model

I. INTRODUCTION

We have now laid down our foundation for ministry and have an overview of basic areas of ministry. In this section we will be discussing the "how to's" of ministry.

We have broken down the ministry (healing process) into five sections to lay down a track to run on. It will be important for you to study and apply this process until it becomes natural to you.

II. FIVE STAGES OF THE MINISTRY PROCEDURE[11]

A. The Five Stage Healing Model – The Interview – Step One

1. This is the gathering of information so we can pray effectively and intelligently.

2. Questioning
   a) Where does it hurt?
   b) How long has it been hurting?
   c) Has a doctor diagnosed it?
   d) What do you feel the problem is?
   e) Other questions etc.

3. Diagnosing on two plains (while listening and gathering facts):
   a. Natural (Empirical).
      (1) Sort according to present/past experience.
      (2) What we see, know, have learned, etc.
   b) Supernatural (Cosmic).
      (1) Sort according to gifts of the Spirit.
      (2) Words of knowledge and wisdom, distinguishing of spirits,
   c) This is NOT a medical interview.
      (1) Remember, we are not physicians.
      (2) Gather only enough information to help you pray, not to discourage you.

4. When interviewing, keep it brief.
   Don't let the person go into a lengthy dialogue, just get the basic facts. Keep control of the interview.

5. The interview is complete when:
   a) You have ascertained cause of condition (i.e. natural, supernatural, social, emotional, sin, etc.).
   b) God has told you what to do.
   Note: If you have not ascertained the cause and God hasn't shown you what to do – pray for affect.

B. Diagnostic Decision – Step Two

1. During this phase we're finding out why this person has this condition so we can deal with the problems not just the condition.

2. In diagnosing the problems people are having, we see they come from the natural and supernatural realm. Let's look at it.
   a) Natural realm:
      (1) Contracted disease.
      (2) Hurt themselves.
      (3) Sin (depression, judgments of guilt, etc.).
      (4) Family problems (financial, relationship, etc.).
      (5) Emotional (psychosomatic illnesses).
      (6) Social (physical problems, harboring ill feelings, unforgiveness).
   b) Supernatural realm:
      (1) Demon (oppression/affliction).
      (2) Demonization.
      (3) White magic/black magic (doctor's diagnosis, parent's pronouncement, occult curses on individual, etc.).

C. Prayer Selection – Step Three

1. Ask ourselves, "What kind of prayer should I pray to help this person?" This is a question you turn toward for a reply or answer.

2. Prayer comes in two forms:
   a) Prayer directed toward God:
      (1) *Petition* (most common) Mark 7:32-25; Acts 9:36-43). Ask for the Holy Spirit's presence and healing.
      (2) Intercessory prayer.
      Cor. 14:14-15 – Prayer with the mind and the spirit.
   b) Prayer from God:
      (1) Command – of faith.
      Luke 4:38, 39; 7:12-15; Mark 3:1-5; John 11:38-44.

(2) Pronouncement – of faith.
Luke 13:10-13; John 4:46-50; Acts 20:7-12.
To demons or spirits:
Rebuke (break their power).
Bind (contain their power).
Expulse (eliminate their presence).

D. Prayer Engagement – Step Four

1. Basics on praying:
   a) Position yourself in front of the person.
   b) Pray with your eyes open and watch what is happening to them.
   c) Dial down. Don't bring things into emotion.
   d) Speak in your normal voice.
   e) Remember you're not the focus. You're not being weighed for performance.
   f) Take a little time. . . wait on God.
   g) Call on the Holy Spirit and work with Him.
   h) Bless what you see the Father doing.

2. Pray while looking for effect:
   a) Warmth
   b) Tingling
   c) Shaking
   d) Peace
   e) Deep breathing, etc.

3. Interview again, when needed.
   a) When you see nothing happening:
      (1) Some people are not in tune with their own body.
      (2) Some people are programmed to failure.
      (3) Some people just don't show any emotion.
   b) When you see something happening – ask them what is going on.

4. Keep open to the Holy Spirit through the gifts to:
   a) Reveal needs and problems.
   b) Change directions of prayer.

5. Stop praying when:
   a) The person you are praying for indicates it is over.
   b) When the Holy Spirit indicates it is over.
   c) When you cannot think of anything else to say.
   d) When you have prayed and it seems you have not gained any ground.

E. Post Prayer Direction – Step Five

1. This phase is helping the person continue and/or keep their healing.
    a) Which can be accomplished by:
        (1) Go and sin no more.
        (2) Make restitution to a person you've hurt.
        (3) Read some Bible scripture.
        (4) Get prayer again and again etc.
        (5) Fight the enemy.
    b) Referral
        (1) Classes being taught at your congregation or ministry (New Christians, Commitment Classes, Foundations, etc.).
        (2) General counseling (call your congregation's office).
        (3) Books or tapes, study guides etc.
        (4) Conferences, seminars, etc.

2. Exhortation to attend prayer gatherings/meetings.

3. Invitation to a home group or peer group ministry involvement.

III. MOST COMMON PITFALLS:

The following are common pitfalls to avoid in our personal ministry skill development.

1. Insensitivity to the person.
2. Preaching and/or dominating.
3. Getting out of control with your hands, face, voice etc.
4. Misdiagnosis due to ignorance.
5. Power loss due to insecurity.
6. Distractions around you drawing away your focus.
7. Spirit of lust or seduction drawing you into a wrong attraction to the one you are ministering to.

IV. HEALING MODEL CURVE

Most of us move through the following steps before we find ourselves fruitful in praying for the sick.

A. Disbelieve:

1. Do not want to know.
2. Do not know.
3. Know and chose not to believe.

B. Open:
Don't believe but you want to. You are moving a step forward.

C. Timid:
You believe, but you are not acting on your faith at this point.

D. Obedient:
You are believing and acting, but not seeing many results thus far.

E. Fruitful:
In this level, you are now believing and acting and seeing positive results. The more you practice, the more success you will see in God.

Reflection Questions
Lesson Three: Five Stage Model

Answers to these questions can be found in the back of the study guide.

Fill in the Blank

1. List the main five points in the Five Stage Healing Model.

    1. _____

    2. _____ 3. _____

    4. _____ 5. _____

2. In your prayer selection, while praying for people, the prayer can come in two forms. What are they? 1. _____

    2. _____

Multiple Choice – Choose the best answer from the list below:

    A.   People   C.   Prayer

    B.   Supernatural   D.   Misdiagnosis

3. In diagnosing the problems people are having, we see they come from the natural and _____ realms.

4. A common pitfall to avoid in personal ministry is _____.

True or False

5. Insensitivity in personal ministry enhances the ministry. _____

6. Asking questions while praying for people is not necessary as long as you listen to the Holy Spirit. _____

7. A command of faith is a prayer from God flowing through you as you respond in obedience. _____

Scripture Memorization

8. Write out and memorize Luke 4:38-39.

Continued on the next page.

9. What was the primary point you learned from this lesson?

Lesson Four:
Using the Word of Knowledge in Healing

I. **DEFINITION OF A WORD OF KNOWLEDGE**

A. **Primary Scripture**
I Cor. 12:7-8 – *But to each one is given the manifestation of the Spirit for the common good. For to one is given the word of wisdom through the Spirit, and to another the word of knowledge according to the same Spirit.*

   1. Given by the Spirit (v. 8) – the distribution of this gracelet (gift) is by the Holy Spirit. Where "liberty" is given to the Holy Spirits presence, this gifting will flow freely.

   2. For the common good (v. 7) – The purpose of this manifestation is to release a touch of God's goodness, care and love to ordinary everyday people.

B. **From Bishop David Pytches**
"This is the supernatural revelation of facts about a person or situation, which is not learned through the efforts of the natural minds, but is a fragment of knowledge freely given by God, disclosing the truth which the Spirit wishes to be made known concerning a particular person or situation."[12]

C. **From Peter Wagner**
The gift of knowledge is the special ability that God gives to certain members of the Body of Christ to discover, accumulate, analyze and clarify information and ideas that are penitent to the growth and well-being of the Body (I Cor. 2:14; 12:8; Acts 5:1-11; Col. 2:2:2-3; II Cor. 11:6).[13]

D. **From Derek Prince**
A word of knowledge is a tiny portion of God's total knowledge supernaturally imparted by the Holy Spirit operated only under God's control.[14]

E. **An Open Book**
There is a vast library of information in the world. Each person's life is an open book before God. He reveals one word off the many pages of or life to help realize that God is near and that He cares.

II. SOME BIBLICAL EXAMPLES

A. General Usage

1. Nathaniel – John 1:43-49.
    Jesus knew Nathaniel's name, what tree he sat under and the condition of his heart. This persuaded him that Jesus was the Messiah.

2. Ananias and Sapphira – Acts 5:1-11.
    Knowledge was granted that a lie was being told and that a portion of the money was being withheld. The result was an increase in the fear of the Lord.

B. During Healing

1. Jesus knows their thoughts – Luke 5:18-26; sin was an issue – v. 20.
    a) In the healing of the paralytic, the condition addressed was a sin issue by which Jesus forgave his sins and the man was healed.
    b) The Pharisees and the teachers of the Law questioned His response to the forgiving of sins, but Jesus already knew what they were thinking– Revealed by a word of knowledge.
    c) Note: The power of the Lord was present to heal the sick – There are places were the flow of healing and revelation function better because the Holy Spirit is there and the people are expectant for Him to move.

2. Jesus knows the Pharisee's thoughts – Luke 6:6-11.
    With the healing of the man with a shriveled hand, the Pharisees were looking for a reason to accuse Jesus for healing on the Sabbath. Again, Jesus knows the evil intent of their hearts through the word of knowledge and responded with a word of wisdom!

3. Jesus knows sickness was caused by a spirit – Luke 13:10-17.
    Jesus addresses the spirit of infirmity in the case of the women who had been crippled for 18 years and healing resulted.

III. WHY DOES GOD REVEAL INFORMATION THROUGH THIS GIFT?

A. It Demonstrates Who He Is
A tiny portion of the vast knowledge of God reveals His nature. It lets us know He is our Creator, Father and Shepherd who cares. It

releases a demonstration of His power and convinces us of His goodness.

B.   It Shows He Knows Who We Are
All the more we realize we are the sheep of His pasture. We are His creation. We are the object of His great love!

C.   It Is a Spiritual Tool
These tools of God's grace are given by the Holy Spirit to heal the Church and release a powerful testimony that Jesus Christ is the same today as He was yesterday.

IV.   WHEN DOES THIS GIFT OCCUR?

A.   When Focused on the Lord

1.   As we worship the Lord and give Him praise He will often "drop" words of knowledge into our mind, heart or awareness. Worship is a key too moving in any of the gifts of the Holy Spirit.

2.   When in prayer wait, pause and let Him commune with you. Remember prayer is a two way conversation.

B.   When Ministering to Someone
Of course! This is exactly when He wants to exhibit this gift! Expect impressions and knowings that go beyond your natural limitations to flow freely.

C.   Interruptions During Daily Activities
Most people have secular jobs. God will take advantage of any time, setting or situation to speak to and speak through us. Remember it is a gift of grace! So expect the unexpected to occur where ever He wants.

V.   HOW DOES THIS OCCUR?

Please refer to the study guide *Releasing Spiritual Gifts* in the lesson "The Gift of Word of Knowledge" for more on this subject.

A.   Dramatic Manners

1.   Dreams
2.   Visions
3.   Angelic Appearances
4.   Audible Voices
5.   Heavenly Visits

B.   Moderate Means

1. Impressions in the mind.
2. Knowings in the heart or "gut".
3. Symptomatic "pain" felt in the body (very common means).
4. Internal voice of the Holy Spirit whispering to you.
5. Drawings of compassion towards someone.
6. Emotional feelings that you know are not your own.
7. Heart sensations in your hand, etc.

C.   Slight or Ordinary Ways

1. A sense of love for someone.
2. A longing to just pray for so and so.
3. A desire for things to go better for a certain individual.
4. A nudge to begin a conversation.
5. Many other simple forms of being led by the Holy Spirit.

VI.   POSSIBLE RESPONSES AND OUTCOMES

A.   Person Responds Positively
Yes! This is what we all want! This will result in faith arising and authentic ministry of a loving God to take place. Healings, deliverances and miracles take place in an atmosphere where faith works through love.

B.   Person Responds, But...

1. Difficulty lies with person receiving ministry.
   In this situation partial healing takes place. Obstacles need identified, soaking prayer is needed, but encourage them to continue to respond.

2. Difficulty lies with person giving ministry.
   In this situation there can be offenses, immature or even bad techniques applied after the word is given. Additional instruction: mentoring, wisdom and guidance needs to be sought.

3. Holy Spirit becomes offended and withdraws.
   God resists the proud but gives grace to the humble. Seek the reason the Holy Spirit has withdrawn and be cleansed with the blood of Jesus and cry out until He returns.

5. Enemy resists God's plan.

Realize, we are in a war and the devil is a thief and tries to stop kill or steal glory that is due God's great name.

C. Person Does Not Respond

1. Difficulty lies with person receiving ministry:
   a) Fear – They simply will not identify themselves due to the bondage of intimidation.
   b) Unbelief – They simply don't believe the word is true for them. After all God couldn't have a word for me!
   c) Misunderstand the word – Accidents occur. At times out of sincere motives people simply have misunderstood the statement they simply did not "hear" it.
   d) Thinks it must be for someone else – Again out of unbelief or an inferiority complex, they shrug off the word and will not acknowledge in their heart that it is for them.

2. Difficulty lies with person giving ministry:
   a) Unclear communication – The person giving the word has simply not communicated clearly or stated it in terms the listener can relate too; is to obscure, too timid, missed the window of opportunity etc.
   b) Missed God – Yes! There is no perfect start! Mistakes do occur. We all miss it at times, we must admit, at times we are wrong. But again seek the Lord for more clarify and flow of revelation.

VII. FOR GOD TO BE GLORIFIED

God's great love for his creation is often demonstrated by the display of the gifts of the Spirit freely flowing in each generation. The amazing thing is that He wants to use us to magnify his Son. Our goal isn't perfection, though we want to be mature. Our goal is that Jesus is magnified and our Father receives glory. What and awesome God we serve. Yes, to God be the glory for the many great things He has done, is doing, and will continue to do!

Reflection Questions
Lesson Four: Using the Word of Knowledge in Healing

Answers to these questions can be found in the back of the study guide.

Fill in the Blank

1. Define in your own words "A Word of Knowledge." _____
   _____
   _____

2. List four ways the Holy Spirit speaks through you? 1. _____
   2. _____ 3. _____ 4. _____

3. What difficulties can occur after a person does respond to a Word of Knowledge. _____
   _____

Multiple Choice – Choose the best answer from the list below:

A.	Gifts	C.	Worship
B.	Obstacles	D.	Church

4. A Word of Knowledge can disclose _____ to the one receiving healing.

5. _____ is a key to operating in the gifts.

True or False

6. The purpose of a Word of Knowledge is to release God's goodness. _____
7. Healing and revelation flow better when the people are expectant. _____
8. Our goal in the use of the gifts is to promote our ministries. _____

Scripture Memorization

9. Write out and memorize I Corinthians 12:7-8.

Continued on the next page.

10. What was the primary point you learned from this lesson?

Section Two:

Releasing God's Healing Power

Lesson Five:
God's Remedy for Rejection

I. THE PROBLEM – REJECTION

When ministering to individuals, the answers to the following basic questions will serve as a starting, helpful tool.

A. Diagnostic Questions:

1. Are they from a divorced or one parent family?
2. Have they had a problem with loneliness or depression?
3. Have they had a problem with rebellion or drugs?
4. Have they ever said, "I wish that I was dead."
5. Have they ever said and meant it, "I hate myself".
6. Have they ever seriously thought of committing suicide?
7. Have they ever attempted to commit suicide?

B. Definition of Rejection:

1. A sense of being unwanted or the sense that although you want people to love you, no one does.

2. The feeling of wanting to be a part of a group but feeling excluded – somehow always being on the outside looking in.

Note: 1 out of 5 people in the U. S. have been seriously affected by rejection. This number could be seriously higher in other cultures and nations.

C. Acceptance – the Opposite of Rejection

Our Father loves us! Jesus Christ has taken our punishment and we are embraced by God not on a basis of our performance but His great love.

D. Scriptures on Rejection:

Isa. 54:6 – *For the Lord has called you, like a wife forsaken and grieved in spirit, even like a wife of one's youth when she is rejected, says your God.*

Prov. 18:14 – *The spirit of a man will sustain his infirmity, but a wounded spirit, who can bear?*

Prov. 18:8; 26:22 – *The words of a talebearer are as crumbs going down into the innermost parts of the belly.*

Rejection is a deep, sometimes hidden, problem. But eventually fruit externally will be born. The deeper the pain and the longer it remains, eventually, there will be numerous other physical and emotional symptoms will become evident.

II. HOW REJECTION BEGINS

A. Possible Examples:

1. Born out of wedlock or some major trauma occurs in life.
2. The Depression Era – "Why do we have to have another child?"
3. "I suppose my father loved me, but he never showed me."
4. Three children and the middle one was overlooked.
5. Comparison – control syndrome. Never satisfied with self or circumstances in life, always comparing themselves to others.
6. Physical characteristics – birthmark, characteristics, weight or the opposite extreme of acceptance can only come if I am the perfect one!
7. The main issue is T I M E – "Our parents gave us things but they never gave us themselves."
   (See the Lesson Six on "Healing the Wounded Spirit" in this study guide for more on this subject.)

III. REACTIONS TO REJECTION[15]

A. Statement:
For every negative emotion, reaction, and attitude there can be a corresponding spirit. Therefore cleansing and healing emotionally as well as deliverance from darkness, breaking of curses etc, must all be addressed for the complete work of salvation to transpire.

B. Two Lines of Reactions to Rejection:

1. Internal descending reactions to rejections:
   a) *Loneliness* – "I am all alone, even in a crowd, and nobody cares."
   b) *Misery/self-pity* – "No one understands me?" or "Why did God make me like this?"
   c) *Depression/moods of gloominess* – "Nothing will ever change and I will be like this the rest of my life."
   d) *Despair/hopelessness* – "It's no good. I might as well give up."
   e) *Death wish* – "I wish I were dead."

      f)   *Suicide* – "What is the good of living? Go ahead, take those pills; take your life."

    2.   External aggressive reactions to rejection:
        a)   *Hardness* – "So what! Who needs them, anyhow?"
        b)   *Indifference* – "I don't care! Nobody is ever going to hurt me again! I'll put up a barrier that no one will ever get through."
        c)   *Rebellion* – "They are against me so I'll be against them! I hate them (God, church, etc.)."
        d)   *Witchcraft* (I Sam. 15:23) Thou shalt have no other gods before me – going into drugs, the occult, etc.
        e)   *Death* (I Chron. 10:13-14) – spiritual and physical.

C. Roots – Not Fruits

We must look for the roots and not just observe the external fruits to have successful ministry. Don't' just minister to the "addiction" level only. Ask what led to the present bondage and dire circumstances? Otherwise the ministry may be likened to cutting down the tree but not dealing with the root issues.

IV. THE SOLUTION

A. The Way of the Cross Leads Home!

Through the cross of Jesus we each have a personal place of belonging. The cross leads to our Fathers arms. Home is the place where we rest in the Father's love.

B. Isaiah 53 – "The Divine Exchange"

Isa. 53:1-4 – *Who has believed our message and to whom has the arm of the Lord been revealed? He grew up before him like a tender shoot, and like a root out of dry ground. He had no beauty or majesty to attract us to him, nothing in his appearance that we should desire him. He was despised and rejected by men, a man of sorrows, and familiar with suffering. Like one from whom men hide their faces he was despised, and we esteemed him not. Surely **He took up our infirmities and carried our sorrows**, yet we considered him stricken by God, smitten by him, and afflicted.*

Isa. 53: 5-8 – *But He was **pierced for our transgressions, He was crushed for our iniquities;** the punishment that brought us peace was upon Him, and **by His wounds we are healed**. We all, like sheep, have gone astray, each of us has turned to his own way; and the Lord has laid on Him the iniquity of us all. He was oppressed and afflicted, yet he did not open his mouth; He was led like a lamb to the slaughter, and as a sheep before her shearers is silent, so He did not* *open his mouth. By oppression and judgment He was taken away. And who can speak of His descendants? For He was cut off from the land of the living;* **for the transgression of my people He was stricken**.

Isa. 53: 9-12 – *He was assigned a grave with the wicked, and with the rich in His death, though He had done no violence, nor was any deceit in His mouth. Yet it was the Lord's will to crush Him and cause Him to suffer, and though the Lord makes His life a guilt offering, He will see His offspring and prolong His days, and the will of the Lord will prosper in His hand. After the suffering of His soul, He will see the light [of life] and be satisfied; by His knowledge my righteous servant will justify many, and He will bear their iniquities. Therefore I will give Him a portion among the great, and He will divide the spoils with the strong, because He poured out His life unto death, and was numbered with the transgressors. For He bore the sin of many, and made intercession for the transgressors* (NIV).

Jesus was punished for our <u>sin</u> that we might be <u>forgiven</u>.
Jesus was wounded for our <u>sicknesses</u> that we might be <u>healed</u>.
Jesus was made <u>sickness</u> itself that we might have <u>health</u>.
Jesus became <u>poor</u> for our sakes that we might have His wealth.
Jesus died our <u>death</u> that we might have His <u>life</u>.

C. Isaiah 53:3 – Jesus Bore Our Sorrows
He was despised and forsaken of men, a man of sorrows and acquainted with grief; and like one from whom men hide their face, He was despised and we did not esteem Him.

The following are examples of how Jesus was rejected:
1. The choice of Barabbas over Jesus was a severe rejection by men. "Away with Him. Crucify Him."
2. His final agony was not by men but by His Father. *My God, My God, why hast thou forsaken Me?* Hab. 1:3 – *Of purer eyes than to behold evil and canst not look on iniquity.*
3. It is my personal conviction that Jesus, our Savior, died of a broken heart for you and me.

D. Acceptance

1. Eph. 1:5-6 – *He predestined us to be adopted as sons through Jesus Christ to Himself, according to the Kind intention of His will, to the praise of the glory of His grace, which He freely bestowed on us in the Beloved.*

2. Eph. 1:5-6 – *He planned in His love that we should be adopted as His children through Jesus Christ – This was His will and*

pleasure that we might praise that glorious generosity of His which he granted to us in His Beloved (J.B Phillips Translation).

3. God does not tolerate us, He fully accepts (embraces and loves) us. He always has time (you never get a busy signal from God).

E. The Practical Steps:

1. Forgive those who rejected you. This is where it all begins!

2. Lay down bitterness, resentment, hatred, and rebellion. Sow a blessing instead of returning evil for evil, insult for insult. (Read Romans 12)

3. Accept the fact that you are accepted in Christ – God accepts you. You have a Father who doesn't just tolerate you, but He loves you! (Eph. 3:14-15; Rom. 8:14-17; John 1:12-13).

4. Accept yourself. Eph. 2:10 – *We are His workmanship (poem), created in Christ Jesus for good works.* It isn't humility to criticize yourself, it is rebellion – Rom. 9:20. Therefore present and break all word curses you have pronounced over your own life.

5. Consider the possibility of prayer for deliverance. Seek counsel from others concerning this issue. (Refer to the study guide on *Deliverance from Darkness* for more on this subject.)

F. Prayer Proclamations
The following are some simple prayer proclamations to help lead the person/people into deliverance.

1. Prayer proclamations to lead people into deliverance:
    "God is my Father. Jesus Christ is my older brother and Savior. I am loved, not hated. I am accepted, not rejected. Heaven is my home. I am a member of the greatest family on earth. My name is Christian. Jesus has freely lavished the Father's love on me."

2. Pronouncement: "I renounce introspection, yet offering myself to the Holy Spirit to be my Judge and the One who convicts me. I confess the sin of rejecting myself." By the blood of Jesus Christ, and by the Father's work of grace, I choose to break the ties with darkness and accept the Father's great love for me!

Reflection Questions
Lesson Five: God's Remedy for Rejection

Answers to these questions can be found in the back of the study guide.

Fill in the Blank

1. Have you suffered with rejection? What were some of the internal and external reactions that occurred to you? _____

_____

_____

2. What was God's answer to such rejection? _____

_____

_____

Multiple Choice – Choose the best answer from the list below:

A.	Feeling	C.	Denial
B.	Evil	D.	Acceptance

3. Rejection can be a _____ of being unwanted and cast aside.
4. _____ is God's remedy for rejection.

True or False

5. If rejection is not dealt with, other physical and emotional symptoms will become evident. _____
6. When open doors of rejection occur, evil spirits will effect negatively ones life. _____
7. Rejection is usually a surface problem and easily dealt with_____.

Scripture Memorization

8. Write out and memorize Ephesians 1:5-6 and 2:10

Continued on the next page.

9. What was the primary point you learned from this lesson?

Lesson Six:
Healing of the Wounded Spirit

Bringing God's healing ointment to past hurts
of the heart, emotions, and remembrances.

Primary Verse:

Proverbs 18:14 – *The spirit of a man will sustain his infirmity; but a wounded spirit who can bear?* [KJV]

The spirit of a man can endure his sickness, but a broken spirit who can bear? [NAS]

I.   MAN – A TRIUNE BEING

A.   Genesis 1:26
*Then God said, "Let **us** make man in **our** image, according to our likeness."*

B.   Genesis 2:7
Then the Lord formed man of dust from the ground and breathed into his nostrils the breath of life; and man became a living being (soul).

C.   James 2:26
For just as the body without the spirit is dead, so also faith without works is dead.

D.   I Thessalonians 5:23
Now may the God of peace sanctify you entirely; and may your spirit and soul and body be preserved complete, without blame, at the coming of our Lord Jesus Christ.

E.   Hebrews 4:12
For the word of God is living and active and sharper than any two-edged sword, and piercing as far as the division of soul and spirit, of both joints and marrow, and able to judge the thoughts and intentions of the heart.

F.   I Corinthians 6:17
But the one who joins himself to the Lord is one spirit with Him. (The triune man joined by the Holy Spirit in union with his spirit now becomes a quad man!)

II. THE CONDITION DESCRIBED

A. Proverbs 15:13

A joyful heart makes a cheerful face, but when the heart is sad, the spirit is broken.

B. Proverbs 14:10

The heart knows its own bitterness and a stranger does not share its joy.

C. Lamentations 3:12-20

Lam. 3:17-19 – *My soul has been rejected from peace; I have forgotten happiness. So I say, "My strength has perished, and so has my hope from the Lord": Remember my affliction and my wandering, the wormwood and the bitterness. Surely my soul remembers and is bowed down with in me.*

D. Hurt, Wounded, Rejected

In the realm of the person's emotions – you fell stepped on, overlooked, crushed, bruised, your life has gone out of you.

E. Quote from John Wimber

"While sickness of the spirit is caused by what we do, sickness of the emotions is generally caused by what is done to us. It grows out of the hurts done to us by other persons or some experience we have been exposed to in the past. These hurts affect us in the present, in the form of bad memories and weak or wounded emotions. This in turn leads us into various forms of sin, depression, a sense of worthlessness and inferiority, unreasoning fears and anxieties, psychosomatic illnesses, etc. Included in this are the present-day effects of the sins of the parents in the bloodline of a person. Thus healing of past hurts touches the emotions, the memories, and the person's bloodline."[16]

F. Quote from John and Paula Sandford

"Christian healing comes then not by making a broken thing good enough to work, but by delivering us from the *power* of that broken thing so that it can no longer rule us, and by teaching us to trust His righteousness to shine in and through that very thing. Those who are healing by restoring the self-image are causing people to trust in something repaired in the flesh, a practice reshaped in their old carnal nature, doomed sooner or later to failure. Whereas the Lord heals by leaving the broken part right in place, overcoming it by its nature. Our trust as Christians can only always be solely in His righteousness in us, as us, for us!"[17]

G. **Dig Up the Root**

A new corn plant and a weed look very similar in nature. We must correctly discern the problem (weed) from the fruitful plant. But we must also do more than break off branches! We must dig up the root so that the fruit will no longer be borne.

H. **All Experts Tend to Agree on Certain Things:**

1. People have problems that sometimes remain untouched by conversion, the baptism of the Holy Spirit, Bible study, and the personal prayer and devotional life of the individual.

2. Hidden in the recesses of the subconscious mind are hurts and wounds that are surrounded by feelings that still adversely affect the person's life in the present.

3. The focus of healing of past hurts is to release those hurtful memories in such a way that they no longer have a negative effect on the present or the future of the individual. This is primarily done through the act of forgiveness.

III. **THE ROOTS OF PERSISTENT HURTS**

A. **The Results of Living in a Fallen World**

1. Incidents of history.
2. Accidents of nature.
3. Disease.
4. Poverty.

B. **Wounds Inflicted by Others**

1. Sins committed against the individual.
   a) Broken relationships.
   b) Demonic access through parental sin.
   c) Criminal behavior.
   d) Prenatal rejections.

2. Performance orientation.
   a) Perspective of society.
   b) Parental expectations.

The Healing Anointing
Lesson Six: Healing of the Wounded Spirit

3. Our own wrong choices and responses.
    a) Personal responsibility.
    b) Bitter-root judgments.
    c) Expectations.

Note: We are a product of our decisions. It's not as important what happens to us in life, but rather how we respond to it.

C. The Place of God's Law

1. The Laws of Retribution.
    a) Honor your father and mother (Deut. 5:16).
    b) Do not judge (Matt. 7:1-2).
    c) Reap what you sow (Matt. 7:17; 13:1-23; Gal. 6:7).
    d) Holding others in bondage (Matt. 18:21-35).

2. The Laws of Healing.
    a) Giving and receiving mercy (Luke 6:36-38).
    b) Confession and repentance of sin (I John 1:8-9).
    c) Ministering forgiveness to one another (John 20:23, James. 5:16).

3. Scriptural Examples of how Wounds Occur.
    a) Erosion of our walls of salvation (Prov. 25:28).
    b) "He who walks in integrity walks securely, but he who perverts his ways will be found out." (Prov. 10:9).
    c) The arrows of words (Jer. 9:8, Prov. 12:18; 18:8).

IV. BIBLICAL CASE HISTORIES[18]

A. Michal – Saul's Daughter
Her attitude toward David affected by Saul's sin (II Sam. 6:12-23 cf. I Sam. 18:28-29).

1. We have already seen Saul's jealousy and bitterness toward David because of God's blessing of success in his life (I Sam. 18). Michal, Saul's daughter, married David.

2. While bringing the ark back to Jerusalem, David worships the Lord with abandonment. When Michal sees this she despises him in her heart (I Sam. 6:16).

3. Michal's reason for despising David was that he embarrassed her by "disrobing in the sight of the slave girls as any vulgar fellow would do" (I Sam. 6:20).

4. But David's reason for her despising him was the real reason. She was jealous of David and his worship of God, because God chose him rather than her father, or anyone from Saul's house, to rule over God's people (I Sam. 6:21).

5. David did not have a heart to rule (as Saul did, which came out in Michal's attitude, I Sam. 6:20, 22), but a heart to serve God and His people.

6. This weakness resulted in a strain in relationships, emotional stress and Michal's barrenness till her death. Nothing more of her is mentioned (I Sam. 6:23).

B. David's Sin Affects His Offspring
(II Sam. 12:7-12; 13:2-29; 16:22, I Kings 11:1-9)

1. David committed adultery and murder, and Nathan prophesied that death and sexual excess would be present in his household (II Sam. 12:7-12). Note that a prophecy is *not the cause* for the things that happen – it is just a *foretelling* of something that will happen.

2. David's son, Ammon, fell in love with Tamar. His emotional state caused physical illness and later affected relationships. Because he couldn't get her legally, he not only committed adultery, but also raped her (II Sam. 13:2-14).

3. Absalom *murdered* Ammon (II Sam. 13:28, 29).

4. Absalom undermined his father's authority and eventually committed adultery with David's concubines (II Sam. 16:22).

5. David's son, Solomon (through the blood line of Bathsheba), became king and disobeyed God by loving many foreign women (who turned his heart from following the Lord). This weakness in Solomon seems to be a result of his parents' sin (I Kings 11:1-9).

C. Joseph and His Adverse Experiences
(Gen. 37:19-28; 39:1-23; 43:6; 45:1-8)

1. Joseph was sold into slavery in Egypt by his brothers. Although he was distressed at the time (42:21), it becomes clear that he forgave his brothers and thus kept himself free from bitterness.

2. His weeping, when he met his brothers in Egypt, brought emotional release. He accepted his brothers without malice.

3. Joseph reinterpreted his hurtful experience in the light of the purposes of God (45:7-8) and he was freed from any effects of the bad memory.

4. His bad experience with Potiphar's wife and his imprisonment did not seem to affect him much. He seemed to forgive easily because he saw these happenings in the light of God's plan (*"The Lord was with him"*, 39:2, 9, 20-23).

D. Two Disciples of the Road to Emmaus
(Luke 24:13-35)

1. It is evident that they were hurt and even disillusioned through the trauma of Jesus' crucifixion (24:19-21).

2. Jesus entered their present dilemma and through conversation, put their recent memories of failure and frustration into a new and positive light.

3. Jesus said that their lack of understanding of the purposes of God and their faithless attitude toward the scriptures had contributed to their despondency (24:25-26).

4. Using the scriptures, Jesus reinterpreted their negative experience into a fundamentally meaningful one, which became a new source of power and hope (24:27).

5. An expanded perspective of Christ's sacrificial death, the victory brought about by His resurrection, and a revelation of Himself as a present reality, brought inner healing to the disciples.

E. Peter's Denial of Jesus
(Matt. 26:33-35, 69-75; Mark 14:27-31, 66-72; Luke 22:31-34, 54-62; John 13:36-38; 18:15-18, 25-27; 21:15-22.)

1. Because Peter set his heart on man's interests, he could not understand why Jesus had to die (Matt. 16:22).

2. He fought to the end in Gethsemane; but when Jesus was led away, Peter followed "afar off" showing his despair and growing disillusionment (Luke 22:54).

3. His faith faltered, and three times he denied knowing Jesus. This caused immediate condemnation and an emotional reaction — bitter weeping and deep depression (Luke 22:62).

4. It is clear that because of the trauma of Jesus' crucifixion, Satan was trying to gain access to the disciples through their emotional crisis; but Jesus had prayed for Peter (Luke 22:31-32).

5. After His resurrection, Jesus personally came to heal Peter's past hurt. He went to where Peter's shame and despair had driven him – fishing! First, through the miracle of the large haul of fish, Jesus brought back to Peter the positive memory of his calling; and thus renewed his hope (John 21:2-7; cf. Luke 5:4-11). Second, around the fire he asked Peter three times, *"Do you love me?"* Jesus reinterpreted Peter's bad memory of a three-fold denial (John 21:9, 15-17; cf. John 18:17-27).

    Jesus simply believed Peter's hesitant, yet honest commitment, *"Lord, you know that I love you"*, and He recommissioned him to *"Feed My sheep"*. This healed Peter emotionally, which in turn renewed him spiritually and relationally.

F. **The Unforgiving Servant**
    (Matt. 18:15-35; 5:23; 24)

    1. Jesus used this parable to illustrate how unforgiveness affects a person's life.

    2. When you have wronged God or someone else (your debt), you must learn to receive forgiveness, no matter how great your sin is (18:23-27).

    3. When someone hurts you or you experience some bad incident (now owing to you), you must learn to forgive unconditionally, no matter what! (18:28-31)

    4. Unforgiveness because of a past hurt can cause all types of torment (18:33-35), spiritual, mental, emotional, physical, and social.

    5. No matter who is in the wrong, if there is any hurt, the onus is always on you to go and put things right by either receiving or giving forgiveness (Matt. 5:23,24, 18:15-22). We must forgive and forget, just as God has forgiven us (Eph. 4:32).

V.   REMEDY

A.   Luke 4:18

Jesus came to *"heal the brokenhearted and set at liberty those who are bruised."* We must acknowledge that Jesus took our pain and carried our sorrows. "See Me," says the Lord!

B.   Turn on the Search Light of the Spirit of God

Jesus called the Holy Spirit the finger of God. Let the Lord specifically point out the bitterness, hurts, wounds, and rejections.

Don't conjure it up. Let Him who sees and knows all, bring it to your remembrance. Pray something like: "Father, in Jesus' name, by the power of the Holy Spirit, drop into my mind the names of the persons you see from my childhood up that I need to forgive."

C.   Forgive, Forgive, Forgive

"Father, in Jesus' name I forgive _____.

1.   The Effects of Unforgiveness (Matt. 18)

   a)   The servant asked for an extension of time, but the master had mercy and forgave the whole debt.
   b)   That servant did not understand, but left the master and began to extract from fellow servants the debts they owed in order to pay back the debt he thought he still owed.
   c)   The master became aware of the servant's behavior and put him in prison to be tormented.
   d)   The result of unforgiveness is, in essence, torment.

2.   What Is Involved in Forgiving Someone?
   Forgiveness is a decision based on an act of the will. In involves:

   a)   Recognizing that I've been totally forgiven.
   b)   Releasing the person from the debt they owe me for the offense.
   c)   Accepting the person as they are and releasing them from the responsibility of having to meet my needs.

   "Lord, I forgive (name of person) for (specifics). I take authority over the enemy, and in the name of Jesus Christ and by the power of His resurrection life; I take back the ground I have allowed Satan to gain in my life because of my attitude with (name). I now choose to give this ground back to my Lord Jesus Christ."

D. Breaking the Power of Inherited Family Spiritual Conditions

"On numerous occasions, we have found people who are the victims of their parents' sin and excesses. We have encountered families that have had a history of alcoholism, sexual perversion, child molestation, and other types of social and emotional abuse. After breaking the power of inherited family and spiritual conditions, we have seen these social behaviors altered, and in a large majority of cases, entirely eliminated. This is true when we are able to minister to the victim as well as the perpetrator of the abuse. I might add that it is almost always in conjunction with other types of therapy." (For reference, see Num. 14:18; Ex. 20:3-5; 34:7; Jer. 32:18; Lam. 5:7; Lev. 26:39,40; Neh. 9:2,16; Deut. 5:9; II Chron. 29:3-9.")[19]

(For more on this subject refer to the study guide – *Deliverance from Darkness*; Lesson Eleven: "Curses; Causes and Cures".)

E. Breaking Soul Ties or Emotional Dependence

"It is important to break the soul ties or emotional dependence on anyone or anything that has had a negative effect. This ministry is usually administered by prayer over the person in which he is pronounced free from the negative dependence that he has had. This type of prayer has proven to be helpful, especially when ministered in conjunction with Bible teaching and counseling that will support a new self-image and a redeemed identity in Christ."[20]

(For more on this subject refer in this study guide to Lesson Seven: "Breaking Emotional Bondages".)

F. Personal Repentance

1. The individual seeking healing must also then turn from any anger or bitterness toward the person(s) having wounded them, and receive forgiveness from God through a brother or sister in Christ (John 20:23).

2. They also must recognize their own responsibility and choice in responding and reacting to the hurt by choosing a self-image that is non-biblical and destructive. By repenting from the sin of faulty self-perception, the individual will open the way for a new image to be formed according to the God's Word (Rom. 12:1-2).

3. Must forgive self. Pray a simple prayer such as:
    "Dear Lord – You have forgiven me and forgotten my sin. I am not higher than You. Therefore, I choose likewise to forgive and release myself and to forget my sin. With Your blood, wash away my guilt and shame and even the remembrance of my sin, in Jesus' name. Amen"

4. We must forgive and release God Himself. Pray a simple prayer such as:

"God, I know that You are holy and cannot sin. You do all things well. My attitude toward You has been one of questioning and bitterness. This is sin. I repent of it. Wash it out of me with Your blood. I realize evil comes from Satan, not from You. Forgive me for blaming You for any of the works of the enemy. I can and do trust you with my life. I trust that You will cause all things to work together for good. Thanks for your abounding love and mercy. In Jesus' name, Amen"

VI. CLOSING INSTRUCTION

A. Loving Sensitivity
Because of the nature of this type of sickness and healing, a loving sensitivity to the person concerned, and to the Holy Spirit and His revelatory gifts, is necessary. We must be careful of superficiality and yet we must avoid needless and hurtful probing in our dealings. We must avoid excess emotionalism.

B. Renew Your Mind!
Instruct them to renew their mind on a regular basis through worship, Bible study, meditation, praying in the Spirit (Rom. 12:1, 2). (For more on this subject refer in this study guide to Lesson Eight: "Transformation by Renewal of the Mind".)

C. Direct Them to Caring Members of the Body of Christ
Just being a part of the body of Christ (and experiencing ongoing growth) will bring all sorts of releases in regard to healing of past hurts. Love steps out on a limb and is vulnerable.

D. Major on the New Nature in Christ
To keep a healthy, biblical balance (and avoid a negative and introverted attitude caused by an overemphasis on inner healing) our focus should be on our new nature in Christ. The Biblical depiction of our new nature is surely a truer, more real and trustworthy evaluation than that provided by our own weaknesses, fears, angers, memories, etc. – not to mention the accuser of the brethren! (Refer to Rom. 8:1-2; 28:35; Eph. 4:20-24; Rev. 12:11, Gal. 2:20).

E. Praise the Lord!
Restore the gate of praise. Offer up an offering of thanksgiving. Jesus has healed your broken heart! (For more on this subject refer to the study guide *War in the Heavenlies*; Lesson Eight: "The High Praises of God in Our Mouths".)

Reflection Questions
Lesson Six: Healing the Wounded Spirit

Answers to these questions can be found in the back of the study guide.

Fill in the Blank

1. Write out Proverbs 18:14 _____

   _____

2. Write out Proverbs 4:10 _____

   _____

3. The focusing on past hurts is to release those _____ memories that affect you negatively.

Multiple Choice – Choose the best answer from the list below:

A.	Forgiveness	C.	Introverted
B.	Unforgiveness	D.	Outward

4. A biblical depiction of our new nature in Christ avoids _____ attitudes.

5. _____ is mandatory in healing emotional wounds.

True or False

6. Sickness of our emotions is caused by what is done to us. _____
7. Hidden in the recesses of the mind can be hurts and wounds that are surrounded by feelings that adversely affect our lives. _____
8. Michal, Saul's daughter, despised her husband David because he disrobed himself. _____

Scripture Memorization

9. Write out and memorize Hebrews 4:12 and I Thessalonians 5:23.

Continued on the next page.

10. What was the primary point you learned from this lesson?

Lesson Seven:
Breaking Emotional Bondages

Severing Soul Ties

I.   A DEFINITION OF TERMS

A.   Quote from James W. Goll

"The breaking of emotional bondages, or commonly called severing *soul ties*, is intrinsically interwoven with the ministries of deliverance, breaking of curses, and healing of the wounded spirit. The common thread is the necessity of receiving and giving forgiveness.

"The breaking of emotional bondages is a three-stage process of forgiving, forgetting, and releasing. It is the severing of emotional, sensual, and/or demonic influences, which hold the individual to the past, and hinders them from walking in and enjoying freedom for today. The severing of these soulish ties is bringing the redemptive work of the cross of Christ into the healing of our memories."

B.   Quote from David Seamands in *Healing of Memories*

"Memories are not simply mental pictures of the past. Rather, they are present experiences of the total person ... feelings, concepts, attitudes, and behavior patterns. Thus, they tend to make us repeat those actions, which accompany the pictures on the screen of our minds.

"This is the way the Bible speaks of memory when it urges God's people to call something to remembrance. Scripture never compartmentalizes us into physical, mental, and spiritual beings, but emphasizes the life of the whole person.

The real tragedy of hurtful memories is not simply the emotional pain they bring or the powerful push from the past we feel within us. Rather, it is because of the pain and the push, we learn wrong ways of relating to people and coping with life. For us to be changed, such memories must be healed so the sanctifying power of the Holy Spirit can work through our daily disciplines."[21]

C.   Quote from John Wimber

"It is important to break soul ties or emotional dependence on anyone or anything that has had a negative effect. This ministry is usually administered by prayer over the person, in which he is pronounced free from the negative dependence that he has had.

"This type of prayer has proven to be helpful, especially when ministered in conjunction with Bible teaching and good counseling that will support a new self-image and a redeemed identity in Christ."[22]

D. Quote from Betty Tapscott in *Inner Healing through Healing of Memories*

"Jesus Christ is the same yesterday, today, and forever. (Heb. 13:8) Time and space mean nothing to Him. He can walk back into our past and heal where we hurt. He wants us to give our past to Him. Phil. 3:13 tells us *to forget the past and look forward to what lies ahead.*

"Some people enjoy living in the past, reliving and going over past hurts, and being a martyr. Jesus will not help these people. But if we want to be made whole, if we really want that inner peace, He is able and faithful to give it to us. Col. 1:13-14 says, *"For He has rescued us out of the darkness and gloom of Satan's kingdom and brought us into the Kingdom of His dear Son, who bought our freedom with His blood and forgave us all our sins."*

"Inner healing is not just going into the past and digging up sordid details. It is not seeing how much garbage we can remember; it is throwing away all the garbage that is there. It is having Jesus shine His divine light in all those dark places where Satan has hidden those hurts and painful memories."[23]

II. PRINCIPLES THAT MAY APPLY
Read the following verses to gain insight and perspective.

A. I Corinthians 6:15-20
Sexual sin carries a consequence different from other sins. These scriptures indicate a sinning "into the body".

B. II Samuel 13:1-22
Amnon, Tamar, and Absalom: the love-hate cycle and the tragedy of sexual trauma. This is a condition true then and true today.

C. Genesis 2:24
Before there can be a proper "cleaving together" as husband and wife, there must be a proper "leaving". Has there been a proper order here? Has there been a "leaving"?

D.   I Samuel 15:23
There must be a severing from dominating soulish powers that come through the spirit of witchcraft and manipulation. This must be exposed and broken in many cases.

E.   II Samuel 6:12-23; I Samuel 18:28-29
Michal – her attitude toward David was affected by Saul's sin.

1.   Saul's jealousy and bitterness towards David came because of God's blessings of success in his life (I Sam. 18). Michal, who was Saul's daughter, married David.

2.   While bringing the ark back to Jerusalem, David worshipped the Lord with abandonment. When Michal saw this, she despised him in her heart (6:16).

3.   Michal's reason for despising David was that he embarrassed her by "disrobing in the sight of the slave girls as any vulgar fellow would do." (6:20).

4.   But David's reason for her despising him was the real reason. She was jealous of David and his worship of God, because God chose him, rather than her father or anyone from Saul's house, to rule over God's people (6:21).

5.   David did not have a heart to rule (as Saul did, which came out in Michal's attitude in 6:20, 22), but a heart to serve God and His people.

6.   This weakness resulted in a strain in relationships, emotional stress, and in Michal's barrenness until her death. Nothing more of her is mentioned (6:23).[24]

F.   Gen. 37:19-28; 39:1-23; 43:6; 45:1-8
Joseph had many adverse experiences:

1.   Joseph was sold into slavery in Egypt by his brothers. Although he was distressed at the time (42:21), it became clear that he forgave his brothers and thus kept himself free from bitterness.

2.   His weeping, when he met with his brothers in Egypt, brought emotional release. He accepted his brothers without malice.

3.   Joseph reinterpreted his hurtful experience in the light of the purposes of God (45:7-8) and was freed from any effects of the bad memory.

4. His bad experience with Potiphar's wife and his imprisonment did not seem to affect him much. He seemed to forgive in light of God's plan (*"The Lord was with him."* 39:2,9,20-23).[25]

III. THE REMEDY

A. Forgiving
This is the first of a three-step process of being set free of these emotional bondages. Receiving and giving forgiveness is covered in detail in the previous lesson on "Healing of the Wounded Spirit."

1. We must learn to properly deal with guilt. There are three types of guilt: true, false, and exaggerated. Essentially, they must all be dealt with in the same manner.

2. Cleanse our conscience – Heb. 9:11-14.
The scapegoat bearing the guilt offering – Lev. 16:20-22.

B. Forgetting

1. Forgetting involves several things: disregarding an offense, removing a judgmental spirit from within, keeping no score of wrongs, and ignoring all the good things I perform.

2. Primary verse: Phil. 3:12-14.
Not that I have already attained it, or have already become perfect, but I press on in order that I may lay hold of that for which also I was laid hold of by Christ Jesus. Brethren, I do not regard myself as having laid hold of it yet; but one thing I do: forgetting what lies behind and reaching forward to what lies ahead, I press on toward the goal for the prize of the upward call of God in Christ Jesus.

3. A specific analysis of forgetting:
   a) Statement of vulnerability
      "I haven't arrived." It is extremely refreshing to come across a very capable, competent people who have retained their vulnerability.
   b) Statement of realism
      "I forget what is behind." When mistreated or hurt by another, the honest, authentic, real person makes the hard choice to forgive and forget.

c)   Statement of determination
"I press on." Those who choose not to forget remain tied to the past. Those who forgive and forget can move ahead to new areas.

4.   Practical response to forgetting:
a)   Forgetting reminds me that I, too, have flaws if others would want to emphasize them.
b)   Forgetting enables me to be big and encouraging, not petty and negative.
c)   Forgetting frees me to live for tomorrow rather than being anchored to yesterday.

C.   Releasing

1.   The third step of this process is vitally important. You must release the control of the individual, group, circumstance, etc. into God's hands. We each have our Abraham-Isaac situations in our lives where we yield the promise back to God. We must relinquish our hopes, fears, hurts, goals, longings, and yearnings, as well as the very person or event.

2.   Matt. 18:27 states:
"And the lord of that slave felt compassion and released him and forgave him the debt."

3.   This releasing may be climaxed in a prayer in which you:
a)   Give the person or event to God.
b)   Release your expectations, hurts, or pains.
c)   Renounce the emotional dependency.
d)   Ask the Lord for a blessing upon the situation.
e)   Grace to turn away and walk free from condemnation.

4.   **FREEDOM** now begins!! But remember, vulnerability is now the new test and the battle of the mind might continue. Enjoy your new peace and believe that **whom the Lord sets free, is free indeed!**

Reflection Questions
Lesson Seven: Breaking Emotional Bondages

Answers to these questions can be found in the back of the study guide.

Fill in the Blank

1. What does it mean when one says to "Severe soul ties" or "break emotional bondages?" _____

   _____

   _____

   _____

2. Define the term "Inner Healing" _____

   _____

   _____

   _____

Multiple Choice – Choose the best answer from the list below:

A.	Offense	C.	Circumstances
B.	Memories	D.	Options

3. For us to be changed, some _____ need to be healed in order for the sanctifying power of the Holy Spirit to move through us.

4. A biblical definition of "Forgetting" could be disregarding or letting go a past _____.

True or False

5. Being vulnerable is part of the restoration process of healing. _____

6. Releasing people in prayer is to giving your expectations, hurts and pain to the Lord. _____

7. Jesus can walk back into your past and heal your wounds and hurts. _____

Scripture Memorization

8. Write out and memorize Colossians 1:13-14

Continued on the next page.

9. What was the primary point you learned from this lesson?

Lesson Eight:
Transformation by Renewal of the Mind

Practical Applications of Romans 12:1-2

I. **PERFECTIONISTIC HANGUPS**

The following is a partial list of the false, absurd, and unrealistic assumptions which contribute greatly to perfectionistic hang-ups and which need changing if healing is to take place.

A. **MYSELF**

   1. I should be liked/approved of/loved by everybody, especially those I consider important to me.

   2. I ought to be able to do anything/everything well – if I can't, it is better not to do it at all or to wait until I can.

   3. I must be perfectly competent and successful in achieving before I consider myself worthwhile and before others do.

   4. I really don't have control over my happiness – it is under the control of others and outside circumstances.

   5. The experiences/influences of the past cannot be changed.

   6. There in only one true/perfect solution for every problem – if I don't find it, I am sunk/lost/will be destroyed.

   7. I ought to be able to make/keep everybody around me happy if I don't, there is something wrong with me.

   8. It is my responsibility to right the wrongs of the world/solve its problems/correct all injustices.

B. **OTHERS**

   1. Others should take care of me/be kind to me/never frustrate me.

   2. Others ought to be able to read my mind and know what I need/want without me telling them – if they can't do this, it is because they don't really like/love me.

C. GOD

1. God only accepts/loves me when He can approve of everything I am/think/feel/say/do.

2. God may accept me as I am, but only because in the future I will never think/feel/say/do anything wrong.

3. God saves me by grace, but only maintains this relationship if I read/pray/witness/serve/do enough.

4. God holds my ultimate salvation in suspense – at the Great White Throne, He will judge me and then determine whether or not I will be given eternal live/heaven.

II. PUTTING ON THE NEW MAN

Here is a partial list of true, realistic, and biblical assumptions to replace the absurd ones. *"Putting off the old and putting on the new"* (Col. 3:9-10) is part of the reprogramming so vital to the healing of our perfectionism.

A. MYSELF AND OTHERS

1. I am a worthwhile person whether I am successful in certain achievements or not.
   a) God has given His opinion of my value and worthwhileness. Psa. 8; Rom. 5:6-8.
   b) God's view on "success" is different from people's view. Luke 10:17-24; I Cor. 1:25-31.
   c) God has eliminated both comparison and competition and asks only "faithfulness" in exercising my particular gift(s). Luke 14:7-11; Matt. 20:1-16; 25:14-30; I Cor. 12:4-27; Rom. 12:6; Acts 5:29.

2. I do not have to be approved/liked/loved by everyone in order to feel secure or lovable.
   a) Some people can't like/love me because of their problems. John 15:18-27; 17:14-19; Gal. 1:10; 4:12-16; I Pet. 4:12-16; John 3:11-13.
   b) Since I am always loved by God (regardless of how some may feel about me), I do not need to be overly concerned about the approval/disapproval of others. John 15:9-10; 17:25-26; Rom. 8; Heb. 13:5-6; I John 4:16-19.

B. GOD

1.   God accepts/loves me even though He does not always approve of everything I do. John 3:16-17; Rom. 5:6-8; I John 4:7-10.

2.   Faith in what He has done for me (in Christ), not perfect performance, is what pleases God and puts/keeps me in a right(eous) relationship with Him.

3.   God, through His Holy Spirit, gives me the assurance of my salvation/eternal life/heaven now – my judgment took place on the cross. My only future judgment will be for service rewards and not for my salvation.   John 3:36; 5:24; I Cor. 3:10-15; I John 3:24; 5:6-13.

III. THE HELMET OF HOPE

A. Primary Verse

1.   Ephesians 6:17
     And take up the helmet of salvation.

2.   Isaiah 59:17
     And He put on righteousness like a breastplate, and a helmet of salvation on his head; And He put on garments of vengeance for clothing, and wrapped himself with zeal as a mantle.

3.   I Thessalonians 5:8
     But since we are of the day, let us be sober having put on the breastplate of faith and love, and as a helmet, the hope of salvation.

B. What Is Hope?
Hope is the positive expectation of something good. One of the missing pieces of the armor of God that we must put on is the grace to guard what we hear and thus what we think through the godly filter of "hope".

Faith is built on the altar of hope (Heb. 11:1). Before we can ever exercise true biblical faith, we must be a people of hope (Rom. 4:18 - 19; 5:2-5; 8:24-25, 15:4; I Cor. 13:13, 15:9; Tit. 2:13; Heb. 6:19; I John 3:3).

Therefore, let the transformation of our mind take place by renewing our minds with God's Word. Then we will be able to do what Philippians 4:8 states:

"Finally brethren, whatever is true, whatever is honorable, whatever is right, whatever is pure, whatever is lonely, whatever is of good repute, if there is any excellence and if anything worthy of praise, let your mind dwell on these things."

Reflection Questions
Lesson Eight: Transformation by Renewal of the Mind

Answers to these questions can be found in the back of the study guide.

Fill in the Blank

1. Examine your own heart in light of point I/A, B, & C in this lesson to see if you fall into any of these unrealistic assumptions of yourself, others or God? Write down what false assumptions were true of you and prayerfully bring them before the Lord for healing.

   _____

   _____

   _____

   _____

   _____

   _____

   _____

Multiple Choice – Choose the best answer from the list below:

A.	Love	C.	Hope
B.	Good	D.	Bad

2. I Thessalonians 5:8 – ... *let us be sober having put on the breastplate of faith and love, and as a helmet, the* _____ *of salvation.*

3. Hope is the positive expectation of something _____.

True or False

4. I do not have to be approved/liked/loved by everyone in order to feel secure or lovable. _____

5. Some people can't like/love me because of my problems. _____

6. God accepts/loves me even though He does not always approve of everything I do. _____

Scripture Memorization

7. Write out and memorize Romans 5:6-8.

Continued on the next page.

8. What was the primary point you learned from this lesson?

Section Three

The Anointing

Lesson Nine:
Compassion – A Necessary Ingredient

I. COMPASSION DEFINED

A. From Webster's Dictionary[26]

Compassion – Sympathetic consciousness of the distress of others, together with a desire to alleviate it.

B. From Vine's Expository Dictionary of New Testament Words[27]

1. Verbs:
   a) *Oikteroo:* to have pity, a feeling of distress through the ills of others, is used of God's compassion – Rom. 9:15.
   b) *Splanchnizomai:* to be moved as to one's inwards, to be moved with compassion, to yearn with compassion, is frequently recorded of Christ towards the multitude and towards individual sufferers – Matt. 9:6 and Luke 7:13.
   c) *Sumpatheo:* to suffer with another, to be affected similarly (English – sympathy), to have compassion upon, Heb. 10:34, of compassion for those in prison, is translated "be touched with" in Heb. 4:15, of Christ as the High Priest.
   d) *Eeleeo:* to have mercy, to show kindness, by beneficence, or assistance – Matt. 18:33.

2. Nouns:
   a) *Oiktrimoso:* the inward parts, the seat of emotion, the "heart," Phil. 2:1; Col. 3:12, "a heart of compassion." It is translated "mercies" in Rom. 12:1.
   b) *Sumpathess:* denotes "suffering with," or "compassionate," in I Pet. 3:8.

C. Statement by Author Ken Blue

"The kind of compassion Jesus was said to have for people was not merely an expression of His will but rather an eruption from deep within His being. Out of this compassion of Jesus sprang His mighty works of rescue, healing, and deliverance."[28]

D. Theme Verses

1. Psalm 145:9
   (NIV) – *The Lord is good to all; He has compassion on all He has made.*

(AMP) – *The Lord is good to all, and His tender mercies are over all His works [the entirety of things created].*

2.   Matthew 9:36
(NAS) – *And seeing the multitudes, He felt compassion for them, because they were distressed and downcast like sheep without a shepherd.*
(AMP) – *When He saw the throngs, He was moved with pity and sympathy for them, because they were bewildered (harassed and distressed and dejected and helpless), like sheep without a shepherd.*

3.   Mark 1:41
(NKJ) – *And Jesus, moved with compassion, put out His hand and touched him, and said to him, I am willing; be cleansed.*
(AMP) – *And being moved with pity and sympathy, Jesus reached out His hand and touched him, and said to him, I am willing; be made clean!*

II. GOD'S COMPASSION TOWARDS US

A. A Revelation of His Nature

What is the nature or character of God like? Can we trust Him? What will He do to us? Does He really care?

1.   Psalm 78:38-39
But He, being full of compassion, forgave their iniquity, and He did not destroy them. Yes, many a time He turned His anger away, and did not stir up all His wrath; for He remembered that they were but flesh, a breath that passes away and does not come again (NKJ).

2.   Psalm 86:15
But thou, O Lord, art a God full of compassion, and gracious, long-suffering, and plenteous in mercy and truth (KJV).

3.   Lamentations 3:21-23
This I recall to my mind, therefore I have hope. It is the Lord's mercies that we are not consumed, because His compassions fail not. They are new every morning: great is thy faithfulness (KJV).

B. Everything He Does Is Related to Who He Is!

1. Testimony of John Wimber – taken from *Power Healing.*
"Lord, I asked, are most people (myself included) afraid to pray for the sick because their understanding of Your nature, who You are and how You work inhibits them? Again, I sensed Him saying, Yes – most people are hesitant, even fearful, to pray for others healing because they misunderstand My compassion and mercy. They know about Me, but they do not always know Me."[29]

Sweeter Than Honey
"It really works, I thought as I found my way toward home, and God used me as a vehicle of his healing mercy. Then I was jolted out of my jubilant mood by an incredible vision.

"Suddenly in my mind's eye there appeared to be a cloud bank superimposed across the sky. But I had never seen a cloudbank like this one, so I pulled my car over to the side of the road to take a closer look. Then I realized it was not a cloudbank, it was a honeycomb with honey dripping out on to people below. The people were in a variety of postures. Some were reverent; they were weeping and holding their hands out to catch the honey and taste it, even inviting others to take some of their honey. Others acted irritated, wiping the honey off themselves, complaining about the mess. I was awestruck. Not knowing what to think, I prayed, 'Lord, what is it?'

"He said, 'It's my mercy, John.' For some people it's a blessing, but for others it's a hindrance. There is plenty for everyone. Don't ever beg me for healing again. The problem isn't on my end, John. It's down there. (For readers who have never had a vision or supernaturally heard God in this fashion, I did not physically hear God speak. I experienced more of an impression, a spiritual sense of God speaking to me. Time proved that what I thought I had heard was true.)

"That was a moving and profound experience; certainly it revolutionized my life more than any other experience I had since becoming a Christian. I have never looked at healing the same way since that day.

"What made this experience so powerful was that it confirmed my newfound conviction, rooted in scripture, that God's abundant grace included diving healing, if only we would believe him for it. I learned this lesson from the story in Mark 9:14-32 of Christ healing a man's son who was possessed by a spirit and as a consequence was mute. After the disciples had failed to heal the boy, the father approached Jesus asking if he could help. Jesus wasted no time in identifying the reason for the disciples' failure: unbelief.

"After explaining to Jesus that his son had been possessed by a spirit since childhood, the man asked, *'But if you can do anything, take pity on us and help us.'* (v.22). Jesus said, *'If you can? Everything is possible for him who believes.'* (v.23). The key to experiencing Gods healing mercy was belief, belief in the God who heals. *I do believe, the father said. 'Help me overcome my unbelief!'* (v.24). With this confession what Jesus called faith as small as a mustard seed in Matthew 17:20, he cast a deaf and mute spirit out of the boy, and the boy was instantly healed.

"What God showed me through scriptures like Mark 9, my first healing, and the honeycomb vision was that He is much greater than I ever imagined Him to be, and with only the smallest act of faith I could experience His compassion and mercy. I also realized that God's mercy is constantly falling on us, because everything that He does is related to what He is: the Father of compassion (mercies, *oiktirmon*) and the God of all comfort, who comforts us in all our troubles. (II Cor. 1:3; Exod. 34:6, Neh. 9:17). Psalm 145:9 says, *'The Lord is good to all. He has compassion on all he has made'*. Titus 3:5 tells us the Lord saves us because of His mercy.

"But too often I did not see God in the fullness of His mercy and grace. I trusted Him to lead me, but I did not trust Him to provide for me; I had faith to receive forgiveness of sins and salvation, but I had no faith for divine healing. I never realized God's mercy was as readily and abundantly available to me as the honey was available to all under the honeycomb.

"Through the honeycomb vision I also understood that my first healing was only the beginning of my experiencing God's mercy if I would only choose to believe and to receive it. In the vision, some people rejoiced, freely received, and freely gave away. The more they gave away, the more they received. There is plenty for everyone, The Lord said. Don't ever beg Me for healing again.

"But others, full of unbelief and skepticism, could not receive the grace, blessings, and gifts of God. They could not see that God's mercy and healing are greater than their understanding of how He works. 'The problem isn't on My end,' the Lord said. 'It's down there.' It is we, not God, who place limitations and unbelief on Gods compassion and mercy. We are invited to cooperate with His Spirit by entering into a diving partnership, a partnership in which He brings direction and provides for healing."[30]

2. Testimony of Mahesh Chavda from *Only God Can Make a Miracle*. "When the Spirit of the Lord comes to us, I realized he anoints us to go and do the works of God the Father: preaching the gospel, healing the sick, and setting the captives free. What did that mean to me? What was the Lord anointing me to do? Where was He sending me?

"The answer, when it came to me in prayer, was surprising. I was regularly asking the Lord, 'Where do you want me to go?' One morning, in 1972, He literally awakened me from sleep with the almost overwhelming conviction that I was to go to work at the Lubbock State School for Retarded Children.

"This was certainly not what I had expected, but the more I sought the Lord for clarity about His call on my life, the stronger the sense grew. 'I am a father to the fatherless,' the Lord seemed to say, 'and I am commissioning you. I am sending you as My ambassador of love to these little ones whom the world has forgotten.'

"A woman in one of the prayer meetings I attended was an employee at the State School. When I told her of my sense from the Lord, she was very excited and immediately arranged for me to have an interview there. The Lubbock State School is located a few miles outside of town. The setting is rather desolate, as is the school itself a cluster of about fifteen small, squat, concrete-and-cinder-block buildings, surrounded by a high chain-link fence. Here and there were a few shrubs and a sapling or two. My first impression was that it looked like a minimum-security prison.

"The children who lived there were tragic cases. Some had been born to mothers who had been using heroin. Some were children of abusive parents. Many were born with some kind of horrible birth defect. All were severely retarded. I remember seeing boys and girls as old as twenty-five, whose mental age was less than one year. Some, despite their size and age, spent all their time in oversized baby cribs where they would remain for the rest of their lives.

"The children who came here truly were forgotten by the world. They were wards of the state. In most cases, they had simply been discarded by their parents. Many were never visited by anyone, not even on their birthday, not even on Christmas. The Lord reminded me of His word in Scripture: Is. 49:15 – *Can a mother forget the baby at her breast and have no compassion on the child she has born? Though she may forget, I will not forget you!*"[31]

Only Love Can Make a Miracle by Mahesh Chavda

"The Lord gave me an overwhelming love for these children. It was hard to explain. It was as though the Lord broke off a little piece of His heart and placed it inside me. I loved those children as though they were my own. Before long even the small didn't bother me anymore.

"I used to work a nine-hour shift in Lily, usually with the ambulatory children – those who were able to get around on their own. When I was off duty, I would go to the non-ambulatory wards just to be with the children there. I had such a love for them. The thought of them having to spend the rest of their lives in those cribs almost broke my heart.

"I knew that God loved them, too, and that He wanted to channel that love through me. I didn't really know what to do with them or even how to pray for them. I used to just hold them and pray quietly in the Spirit. Often I would sit in a rocking chair with one of them for hours, just praying and singing in tongues.

"One little girl especially touched my heart. Her name was Laura. Laura's mother had been using hard drugs during pregnancy, and she had been born blind and severely retarded. I used to rotate through the different non-ambulatory wards on my after-hours visits, but in time I began to gravitate more and more to little Laura. She was so precious to me.

"One day I had occasion to go into Laura's ward during the day. It had been several weeks since I had started holding her and praying with her. As I approached her crib, she turned toward me and stretched out her hands to welcome me! There were a number of staff members nearby. They were amazed. They kept saying to each other, 'Did you see that?' Laura had never shown any outward response to anyone before, not even to being touched. Now she was responding to me from across the room. Could it be that she was gaining her sight? Could it be that the Lord was healing her through my prayers?

"Not long after this, I had a similar experience with a little boy who had been born with a terrible birth defect. His spine was deformed so that he was unable to sit up. Again, after I had been praying with him over a period of several weeks, he suddenly became able to sit up. His back was healed!

"As far as I can recall, I never once specifically prayed that these children be healed. I had prayed that way for my mother because I felt the Lord had told me to. Other than that, prayer for healing was not something I was accustomed to doing. When I was with the children, I would simply hold them and pray that the Lord would somehow enable them to experience His love through me. I was as surprised as anyone when they started getting better.

"I was already learning many lessons in my school of the Spirit. My initial encounter with Sister Marsha had already taught me that the Lord works through men and women of every Christian background. Here I was, a Hindu boy converted to Christianity by Baptist missionaries, learning about the things of the Spirit from a Roman Catholic nun! Since them, I have never disdained any of the churches, nor had any problem with learning about the Lord through any of them.

"Now I was learning that the power of God was to be found in the love of God. When the Lord sent me to the State School, he did not say, I am sending you as My ambassador of power or of miracles. He said, "I am sending you as My ambassador of love." That was the way I saw myself and that was the way I prayed for the children – that the Lord would make His love real to them. The healings came almost as a by-product. I learned that only love can make a miracle.

"I learned another lesson, too, that has been very important to me through the years. It is that when I am confronted with human tragedy and suffering, I never ask the Lord, 'Why?' It was often very tempting, when I was sitting there in my rocking chair, holding an eight-year-old child with serious physical defects and severe mental impairment, to get upset with God. How could You let this happen? What kind of God are You, anyway?

"I came to see that this kind of thinking flows from a humanistic frame of mind, not from a genuine knowledge of God. Who was I to stamp my foot and shake my fists at God, as though He were not measuring up to my standards? I was His ambassador, not the other way around. It was not up to me to judge Him.

"During those long hours of prayer, the Lord would say to me, 'Just praise Me'. As I would do so, singing or praying quietly in tongues, He would help me see that the tragedy and heartache all around me was the work of the evil one, of Satan, not of the Lord. It is Satan who seeks to kill, and destroy human beings. God desires their good. We, as God's ambassadors, are commissioned to bring His love into every painful situation so that He can overcome the work of the devil."[32]

3. Micah 7:18-20.
    Who is a God like Thee, who pardons iniquity and passes over the rebellious act of the remnant of His Possession? He does not retain His anger forever, because He delights in unchanging love. He will again have compassion on us; He will tread our iniquities under foot. Yes, Thou wilt cast all their sins into the depths of the sea. Thou wilt give truth to Jacob and unchanging love to Abraham, which Thou didst swear to our forefathers from the days of old.

III. GOD'S COMPASSION THROUGH US

A. Opening Our Eyes to Look and See
Luke 15:20
Compassion erupts out of the father towards his prodigal son while he was still far away.

The Samaritan looked upon the man along the road and had compassion upon him (Luke 10:33).

B. Following in the Priestly Processional
Hebrews 5:1-4
He can have compassion on those who are ignorant and going astray, since He himself is also beset by weakness (v.2, NKJ).

We are called to a priestly ministry. Even as the priests under the Old Covenant identified with the weaknesses of others, so are we called to do for our generation.

C.   **Testimonies in Our Time**

1.   "Do not give up!" The testimony of a healing in Haiti. Mahesh Chavda for a crusade in Haiti. The evangelistic crusade went 5 nights. Each night a little girl brought her grandmother to be prayed for. For four nights in a row this transpired. Each night the power of God touched her but nothing visibly changed. The fifth night when she was prayed for, a miracle occurred. The 77-year-old woman who had been blind since birth could now see. PTL! Her persistence paid off.

2.   What is your experience?   Remember, it is His work and His Divine grace!

IV.   BE IT AND DO IT!

A.   **Know Who You Are – Then You Know What To Do!**
When we begin to be sensitive to the needs of others and to minister to them in this way, the ruins of the body of Christ will begin to be rebuilt and repaired and a body, which has been desolate for many generations, will be restored. This type of ministry takes a real laying down of your life, your desires, and what is convenient for you to help and minister to someone else.

1.   Isaiah 61:6 – this is who we are.
2.   Isaiah 61:1-3 –this is what we do.
3.   Isaiah 61:4 – this is the result.

B.   **Demonstrate What You Have Been Given**

1.   Zechariah 7:9-10
Thus has the Lord of hosts said, Dispense true justice and practice kindness and compassion each to his brother; and do not oppress the orphan, the stranger or the poor; and do not devise evil in your hearts against one another.

2.   Jude 22
And of some have compassion, making a difference (KJV).

Reflection Questions
Lesson Nine: Compassion – A Necessary Ingredient

Answers to these questions can be found in the back of the study guide.

Fill in the Blank

1. Define the Greek term – *Splanchnizomai* _____
   _____

2. Define the Greek term – *Oiktero* _____
   _____

3. Define the Greek term – *Sumpatheo* _____
   _____

Multiple Choice – Choose the best answer from the list below:

A.	Bondage	C.	Peace
B.	Eruption	D.	Identify

4. Compassion is an _____ of love from deep within your soul.
5. We are called to _____ with the weakness of others.

True or False

6. Compassion helps restore the body of Christ. _____
7. Insensitivity is an ingredient of compassion. _____
8 .In Luke 10 it was the Levite who had compassion on the injured man. _____

Scripture Memorization

9. Write out and memorize Psalm 145:9; Mark 14:1.

Continued on the next page.

10. What was the primary point you learned from this lesson?

Lesson Ten:
Understanding the Anointing

I. **OPENING COMMENTS**

A. **Prophetic Word – By Rodney Howard-Browne in July, 1991:**
"The great men and women of God that I am using in the earth today are not being used because they are something special. I am using them for one reason and one reason alone. It's because they've touched Me and I have touched them."[33]

B. **Key Statement**
The anointing is the presence and the power of God manifested. It is the manifested presence of God.

C. **Primary Verse – Isaiah 10:27**
It shall come to pass in that day that his burden will be taken away from your shoulder, and his yoke from your neck, and the yoke will be destroyed because of the anointing oil (NKJV).

D. **Other Scriptures**

1. Luke 4:14-19 – *And Jesus returned to Galilee in the power of the Spirit; and news about Him spread through all the surrounding district. And He began teaching in their synagogues and was praised by all. And He came to Nazareth, where He had been brought up; and as was His custom, He entered the synagogue on the Sabbath, and stood up to read. And the book of the prophet Isaiah was handed to Him. And He opened the book, and found the place where it was written; "The spirit of the Lord is upon Me, because He has anointed Me to preach the gospel to the poor. He has sent Me to proclaim release to the captives, and recovery of sight to the blind, to set free those who are downtrodden, to proclaim the favorable year of the Lord."*

2. Luke 5:15-17 – *Yet the news about him spread all the more, so that crowds of people came to hear him and to be healed of their sicknesses. But Jesus often withdrew to lonely places and prayed. One day as he was teaching, Pharisees and teachers of the law, who had come from every village of Galilee and from Judea and Jerusalem, were sitting there. And the power of the Lord was present for him to heal the sick* (NIV).

3.   I John 2:20 – *But you have an anointing from the Holy One, and all of you know the truth.*

4.   I John 2:27 – *And as for you, the anointing which you received from Him abides in you, and you have no need for anyone to teach you, but as His anointing teaches you about all things, and is true and is not a lie, and just as it has taught you, you abide in Him.*

II. DEFINING THE ANOINTING

A. The Anointing Breaks the Yoke

1.   Yoke defined
    a)   Heavy, oppressing, burden that weighs you down.
    b)   Something that is put upon you (sometimes to join you with another) for the purpose of channeling you into usefulness.

2.   We need the right yoke
Matt. 11:29-30 – (Jesus said) *Take My yoke upon you, and learn of Me; for I am meek and lowly in heart; and ye shall find rest unto your souls. For My yoke is easy, and My burden is light* (KJV).

B. What Is the Anointing?

1.   In Hebrew – "anointing" and "Messiah" come from the same root.
2.   The Greek word for Christ, *Cristos*, means "the anointed one".

C. What It Means to be Consecrated

1.   Consecration means that something is consecrated, set apart, to God. Man sets it apart to be available to the Lord.
2.   Consecration also means that something is consecrated by God. God sets it apart for man through supernatural enablement.

III. THE ANOINTING AND JESUS

A. Philippians 2:5-11
Have this attitude in yourselves, which was also in Christ Jesus, who, although He existed in the form of God, did not regard equality with God a thing to be grasped, but emptied Himself, taking the form of a bondservant, and being made in the likeness of men. And being found in appearance as a man, He humbled Himself by becoming obedient to the point of death, even death on a cross. Therefore also God highly exalted Him, and bestowed on Him the name which is above every

name, that at the name of Jesus every knee should bow, of those who are in heaven, and on earth, and under the earth, and that every tongue should confess that Jesus Christ is Lord, to the glory of God the Father.

Points to Remember:

1. In Phil. 2:5-11, we find the seven steps of humiliation and the seven steps of exaltation. The way up is the way down.

2. Jesus performed His first miracle at the wedding at Cana of Galilee (John 2:11). This was followed by His water baptism and anointing of the Holy Spirit, at which Mt. 3:17 says that God declared about Jesus, – *This is My beloved Son, in whom I am well pleased.* God the Father was pleased with Jesus as His Son at age 14, 18, 21, 25, and 28 years old!

    This was before Jesus had ever done a miracle. The Father was pleased with His Son for who He was and not just for what He would accomplish. The same is true for us!

B. Acts 10:38

You know of Jesus of Nazareth, how God anointed Him with the Holy Spirit and with power, and how He went about doing good, and healing all who were oppressed by the devil; for God was with Him.

C. John 3:27-36

John answered and said, "A man can receive nothing, unless it has been given him from heaven. You yourselves bear me witness that I said, 'I am not the Christ,' but 'I have been sent before Him.' He who has the bride is the bridegroom; but the friend of the bridegroom, who stands and hears him, rejoices greatly because of the bridegroom's voice. And so this joy of mine has been made full. He must increase, but I must decrease. He who comes from above is above all; he who is of the earth is from the earth and speaks of the earth. He who comes from heaven is above all. What He has seen and heard, of that He bears witness; and no man receives His witness. He who has received His witness has set his seal to this, that God is true. For He whom God has sent speaks the words of God; for He gives the Spirit without measure. The Father loves the Son, and has given all things into His hand. He who believes in the Son has eternal life; but he who does not obey the Son shall not see life, but the wrath of God abides on him".

Note especially v. 34, *For He whom God has sent speaks the words of God for He gives the Spirit without measure.* This is a word to the body, not just to one individual and not just to one stream.

D. Jesus and the Five-Fold Ministry Gifts (Eph. 4:11-12)

1. Heb. 3:1 – *Consider the Apostle and High Priest of our profession, Christ Jesus* (KJV).

2. John 4:19 – spoken by the woman at the well, *"Sir, I perceive that thou art a prophet."* (KJV)

3. Luke 4:18a – *The Spirit of the Lord is upon me, because he hath anointed me to preach the gospel to the poor...* (KJV).

4. Pastor
   a) I Pet. 5:4a – *And when the chief Shepherd shall appear...* (KJV).
   b) John 10:14a – *I am the good shepherd...* (KJV).

5. Matt. 9:35a – *And Jesus went about all the cities and villages, teaching in their synagogues...* (KJV).

Jesus, obviously, functioned in all five of these anointed ministries as the Chief Apostle, Prophet, Evangelist, Pastor, and Teacher. Virtue and power came forth from Jesus to the people. He flowed in the anointing.

IV. WHAT IS THE ANOINTING OF CHRIST?

A. It Is the Measure of the Gift of Christ
Eph. 4:7,11 – But to each one of us grace was given according to the measure of Christ's gift ... And He gave some as apostles, and some as prophets, and some as evangelists, and some as pastors and teachers...

B. It Is God's Supernatural Ability Upon Man
It can be both a residential grace gift of the Holy Spirit given from God now within the person or it can be a circumstantial gifting occasionally coming upon a person.

C. It Is Like the Wind
You cannot see the anointing, or the manifested presence of Christ, but you can see its results. In that manner, it is like a wind. You don't know where it comes from or in some dimensions where it going, but you can watch the effects as it passes by.

D. It Is God's Electricity

Thomas Edison experimented on how to tap into a natural power source. We, likewise, through trial and error, come to learn how to tap into that which is freely available, and how to channel it into a useful purpose.

E. It Is a Person – Christ Himself!

It is not as much "what" is the anointing, as it is "Who" is the anointing! The anointing is the person of Jesus Christ manifesting Himself by grace.

V. WHAT ABOUT ME?

A. Three Primary Types of Ministry

In the Old Testament, there were three primary types of ministry anointings. They are the:

1. Prophet
2. Priest
3. King

B. Gracelets (Gifts) of God

In the New Testament, we find that we each receive a special grace package. According to I Pet. 4:10 –11, *As each one has received a special gift, employ it in serving one another, as good stewards of the manifold grace of God. Whoever speaks, let him speak, as it were, the utterances of God; whoever serves, let him do so as by the strength which God supplies; so that in all things God may be glorified through Jesus Christ, to whom belongs the glory and dominion forever and ever. Amen.*

C. Each Given the Spirit

I Corinthians 12:7 – tells us, *But to each one is given the manifestation of the Spirit for the common good.*
This indicates that each believer receives the gifts of the Holy Spirit. This refers to "you" personally!

VI. WHAT ABOUT HIM?

A. He Shall Be In You

1. John 14:16-17 – ... *He abides with you and will be in you*
2. John 7:38 – ... *From his innermost being shall flow rivers of living water.*
3. John 4:14 – ... *shall become in him a well of water springing up to eternal life.*

B. II Corinthians 1:21-22

Now He who establishes us with you in Christ and anointed us is God, who also sealed us and gave us the Spirit in our hearts as a pledge.

Not only is there the "wind of God" that comes externally upon and around us, but there is the "well of God" within us to draw forth from.

VII. CLOSING

A. Testimony of James W. Goll, July 1984

This was an experience where the Lord said to me, "I am now giving you two drops of My anointing oil. One is for you and the other you are to give to your wife. But a day will come later when I will pour the anointing oil upon your head."

B. Prophecy Given to Kenneth Hagin[34]

This portion was taken from the book, *Understanding the Anointing*, by Kenneth E. Hagin.

We're moving up now into the things of God.
And I heard the Spirit say,
There will come further revelation along these lines,
but it has to come line upon line,
precept upon precept.
And as it comes,
men and women will flow with the Spirit,
and there will be such a manifestation of
My power and My glory and My Spirit and My anointing
in these days – in this decade in which you live –
that it will startle men.
Now many who are on the fringes of the move of God
will draw back and say,
"Ahhh, that's fanaticism. No, we can't go with that.
We believe in doing things in a nice, sedate manner."

Never, never, never feel resentment
toward others who may criticize you,
or who may speak against you.
Never allow the least bit of resentment
or ill will, or bad feelings, but walk on.
Walk on in love.
Walk on in power.
Walk on in the Spirit.

Walk on with the Lord,
and He'll come unto thee and
manifest Himself unto thee.

And it is even written in the Holy Scriptures
that His coming unto us shall be as the rain.
And so the Holy Ghost will fall, and the power of God will
be in manifestation, and great shall be the reward thereof.
And many shall be blessed,
and great and good days stand just ahead.
Walk on. Yea, ye shall see, for the glory of the Lord
shall appear unto thee.
But most will move with the Spirit,
and all will acknowledge,
"There are miracles happening over there.
Guess God just saw fit to have mercy on them."
But no, they saw fit to flow with God.
And they saw fit to go with God,
for He is at work in the earth tonight
and He indwells His Body, which is the Church,
which is the house of God.
And His glory will fill that temple.

Many will say, "I just don't go along with those things.
We have a pretty good church here.
God has put His approval upon us."
But yea, saith the Lord of Hosts, I only put my approval upon
that which lines up with my Word.
Get into the Word and let the Spirit open the Word to you.
Not only unto your mind, but get the revelation of it in your spirit.
And your spirit will be more alive unto the things of God.
And He – through your spirit – will be able
to teach you, and admonish you, and direct you.

Reflection Questions
Lesson Ten: Understanding the Anointing

Answers to these questions can be found in the back of the study guide.

Fill in the Blank

1. Define the word "Anointing". _____
   _____
   _____

2. Define the biblical word "Yoke". _____
   _____

Multiple Choice: Choose the best answer from the list below:

A.	Gift	C.	Proclaim
B.	Anointing	D.	Teaches

3. I John 2:20 – *But you have an _____ from the Holy One, and all of you know the truth.*

4. I John 2:27 – *As for you, the anointing you received from Him remains in you, and you do not need anyone to teach you. But as His anointing _____ you about all things and as that anointing is real, not counterfeit just as it has taught you, remain in Him.*

True or False

5. The anointing is the manifest presence of the Lord. _____

6. Gifts are given for the common good (I Cor. 12:7-9). _____

7. Each one must learn how to flow in the anointing. _____

Scripture Memorization

8. Write out and memorize Isaiah 10:27 (KJV or NASB).

Continued on the next page.

9. What was the primary point you learned from this lesson?

Lesson Eleven:
Cooperating with the Anointing

Increasing and Releasing,
Yielding to and Wooing the Holy Spirit

I. CALLING FOR THE SPIRIT'S PRESENCE

A. Concerns

Some have concern over this phenomenon. Is it commanding God? Or inviting the Spirit? I believe it is any/all of the following five things:

1. An intercessory plea.
2. A welcome mat being put out.
3. A declaration of faith.
4. An acknowledgment of what is already occurring.
5. A proclamation of "what is coming."

B. Praying for the Holy Spirit to be Released

Although at times the Spirit "fell" sovereignly and spontaneously (Acts 2:2; 10:44), there were times when the disciples prayed for the Holy Spirit to be released. Acts 4:31 states – *And when they had prayed, the place where they had gathered together was shaken, and they were all filled with the Holy Spirit.*

C. Proceeding with Confidence

We may proceed to do this with confidence because:

1. The Scriptures teach us that we can ask for the Holy Spirit (Luke 11:13).
2. The Church needs power. (The Church was first empowered this way – Acts 1:8; 2:4.)
3. Church growth in Acts was triggered with a manifestation of God's power through signs and wonders (Acts 5:12, 14).
4. Paul, despite brilliant reasoning, rated demonstrations of God's power more highly than just preaching the gospel. (I Cor. 2:4)
5. Miracles, signs, and wonders were wrought by the power of God to confirm the preaching of the gospel (Mark 16:20; Acts 14:3; Heb. 2:3-4).
6. The anointing of power through the Holy Spirit accomplishes the "release" of the gifts of the Spirit and allows God to initiate spiritual ministry (I Cor. 12:11).

7. Experientially, it releases blessing, anointing, and ministry. The Gospel is confirmed, the Kingdom of God extended, and Jesus is magnified.[35]

D. Realize That It Can Be An "Uncomfortable" Ministry Style

1. Accept that this is an "uncomfortable ministry style." (And get used to it.)
2. God is unpredictable.
3. God can often be untidy. *Let all things be done decently and in order.* (I Cor. 14:40, KJV). God's idea of order is not necessarily man's idea of order, however.
4. We must let God be God!

II. FALLING IN THE SPIRIT

A. Terminology
Terms used biblically and throughout church history for this phenomenon.

1. "Falling"
2. "Being slain"
3. "Slayed/slain in the Spirit"
4. "Resting in the Spirit"
5. "Swooning"
6. "Zapped"
7. "Overcome by the Spirit"
8. "Overpowered"
9. "Rapt in ecstasy"
10. "Struck down"
11. "Fainting"
12. "The "glory fall"
13. "Having a glory fit"
14. "Prostration"
15. "Deep sleep"
16. "Falling under the power"

B. Scriptural References

1. The prophets sometimes fell as the Spirit came upon them, giving them a vision, burden, or message from God.
   a) Ezek. 1:28b – ... *When I saw it (the glory of the Lord), I fell facedown, and I heard the voice of one speaking* (NIV).

    b)   Dan. 10:9 – *Then I heard him speaking, and as I listened to him, I fell into a deep sleep, my face to the ground.* (NIV)

    c)   Rev. 1:17a – *When I saw him, I fell at his feet as though dead* (NIV).

2.   The priests, in the Old Testament, appear to have fallen under the "cloud of God's presence" as they worshipped the Lord, as recorded in II Chron. 5:14.

3.   The disciples who accompanied Christ fell on their faces before their transfigured Lord (Matt. 17:6).

4.   When people were delivered from demons, they often fell under God's power – so it seems (Mark 3:11; 9:26-27).

5.   Saul was thrown to the ground with all his companions when he saw a light from heaven on his journey to Damascus (Acts 26:14; Refer also to Acts 9:4).

6.   An unbeliever coming into the company of believers where gifts are in operation ... will fall down and worship God, exclaiming, 'God is really among you!' (I Cor. 14:25b, NIV).

7.   The crowd at Jesus' arrest drew back when Jesus said "*I am He,*" and fell to the ground. (John 18:6).[36]

C. Contemporary Examples

There are numerous examples throughout church history of the manifestations of the Holy Spirit occurring. Francis MacNutt has written an excellent book, *Overcome by the Spirit*, which recounts these experiences.

1.   Teresa of Avila.[37]
    The sixteenth-century saint Teresa of Avila, writes in her autobiography:
    "While seeking God in this way, the soul becomes conscious that it is fainting almost completely away, in a kind of swoon, with an exceeding great and sweet delight. It gradually ceases to breathe and all its bodily strength begins to fail it: it cannot even move its hands without great pain; its eyes involuntarily close, or, if they remain open, they can hardly see .... He can apprehend nothing with the senses, which only hinder his soul's joy and thus harm rather than help him. It is futile for him to attempt to speak: his mind cannot form a single word, nor, if it could, would he have the strength to pronounce it. For in this condition all outward strength vanishes, while the strength of

the soul increases so that it may the better have the fruition of its bliss.

"This prayer, for however long it may last, does no harm; at least it has never done any to me, nor do I ever remember feeling any ill effects after the Lord has granted me this favor, however unwell I may have been: indeed, I am generally much the better for it. What harm can possibly be done by so great a blessing? The outward effects are so noteworthy that there can be no doubt some great thing has taken place: we experience a loss of strength but the experience is one of such delight that afterwards our strength grows greater."

Teresa, of course, was an extraordinary saint; yet her description shares many elements of what we find happening to ordinary Christian people (or even notable sinners) at our services:

a)   Her body can hardly move.
b)   She is not totally unconscious but is aware only vaguely of what is going on around her.
c)   Hours can elapse while she is in this condition.
d)   The basic thrust of the experience is interior; the body is simply out of it as the person's energy focuses on what is happening in the spiritual realm.
e)   Healing and physical well-being are a common result.

2.   Francis MacNutt[38]
Testimonies from Francis MacNutt's ministry:

a)   "In 1975 when Francis MacNutt prayed over me in a healing service I rested in the Spirit for two hours and twenty minutes. During that time I not only realized that I had not forgiven certain people, a fact I was unaware of before, but I also learned more about the nature and demands of Christian forgiveness while lying on the ground there than I had ever understood from talks or books. The Holy Spirit gave me a much deeper insight on this subject, which I regard as one of the major spiritual blessings of my life."

b)   "I asked for the spirit of anxiety to be taken away from me and the infilling of His peace. As you prayed over me a great power forced me back. I was trying to stay on my feet; as the force became less I could see a bright light and I was as if caught up in it. I've never seen anything so bright. I singing joyfully as I witnessed this brightness.
The next morning I awoke in a spirit of peace I have never known, and I could smell the scent of roses ... I was in that state of peace for quite a few days."

3. David Pytches.[39]
    Bishop David Pytches recounts the following story:
    "Some two years ago a boy came forward for prayer in St.
    Andrew's. He had a history of epilepsy, was small, hyperactive
    and behind in his schoolwork due to this affliction. The Holy
    Spirit was invoked to come upon him, and a few seconds later
    he fell to the floor. He looked so white and still that at least one
    person thought he had died and was only comforted by reflecting
    that when Jesus ministered to an epileptic he fell and appeared
    like a corpse (Mark 9:26). After a while the boy seemed to revive
    and his parents took him home and put him to bed. He slept for
    fourteen hours; in fact, he slept so much the following week that
    he could not go to school. Since that day he has never had a
    single "fit". He has grown several inches. By the time this is in
    print he will have taken several levels at school. His doctor has
    just seen him and says there is no reason why he should not
    drive a motorbike. This was the Lord's doing and marvelous in
    our eyes!"

4. John Tauler.[40]
    "One day, as John Tauler was praying, he heard with his bodily
    ears a voice that said: 'Stand fast in thy peace and trust in God.
    And remember that when He was on earth in His human nature,
    when He cured men of bodily sickness, He also made them well
    in their souls.' The moment these words were spoken, he lost all
    sense and reason, and knew not whether he was carried away
    nor how. But when he came to his senses again, he found a
    great change had taken place in him. All his interior and his
    outward faculties were conscious of a new strength; and he was
    gifted with clear perceptions of matters that had before been
    very strange and alien to him."

5. John Wesley.[41]
    From Wesley's journal:
    "Monday, Jan. 1, 1739 – Mr. Hall, Kinchin, Ingham, Whitefield,
    Lane, with about sixty of our brethren. About three in the
    morning, as we were continuing instant in prayer, the power of
    God came mightily upon us, insomuch that many cried out for
    exceeding joy, and many fell to the ground. As soon as we were
    recovered a little from that awe and amazement at the presence
    of his Majesty, we broke out with one voice, 'We praise thee, O
    God; we acknowledge thee to be the Lord.'"

6. Quakers.[42]
    "...Two Quakers, Audland and Camm, preached conversion in
    Bristol and some of the congregation fell to the ground and

foamed at the mouth. But Wesley's ministry became the most celebrated (and controversial) because of the dramatic outbreaks among his audiences.

Here are some descriptions of what happened:
a)   "He was preaching at Bristol, to people who cried as in the agonies of death, who were struck to the ground and lay there groaning, who were released (so it seemed) with a visible struggle then and there from the power of the devil."
b)   At Limerick in 1762:
      "Many more were brought to the birth. All were in floods of ears, cried, prayed, roared aloud, all of them lying on the ground."
c)   At Coleford in 1784:
      "When I began to pray, the flame broke out. Many cried aloud, many sank to the ground, many trembled exceedingly."

7.   George Whitefield.[43]
      "Whitefield's preaching was ordinarily accompanied by people toppling over: some were struck pale as death, others were wringing their hands, others lying on the ground, others sinking into the arms of their friends.

      Under Mr. Whitefield's sermon, many of the immense crowd that filled every part of the burial ground, were overcome with fainting. Some sobbed deeply, others wept silently ... When the sermon was ended people seemed chained to the ground."

8.   Charles Finney[44]
      From the ministry of Charles Finney:
      "The first time people were overcome by his preaching occurred one afternoon in Utica, New York, when, fifteen minutes into his sermon, some 400 people fell off their chairs onto the floor. As Finney himself commented later, In every age of the Church, cases have occurred in which persons have had such clear manifestations of Divine truth as to prostrate their physical strength entirely. This appears to have been the case with Daniel. He fainted and was unable to stand. Saul of Tarsus seems to have been overwhelmed and prostrated under the blaze of Divine glory that surrounded him. I have met with many cases where the physical powers were entirely prostrated by a clear apprehension of the infinitely great and weighty truths of religion.

      "With respect to these cases I remark: that they are not cases of that objectionable excitement of which I spoke in my former letter. For in these cases, the intelligence does not appear to be stultified and confused, but to be full of light. Manifestly there is no such effervescence of the sensibility as produces tears, or any of the usual manifestations of an excited imagination, or deeply moved feelings. There is not that gush of feeling which distracts the thought; but the mind sees truth, unveiled, and in such relations as really to take away all bodily strength, while the mind looks in upon the unveiled glories of the Godhead. The veil seems to be removed from the mind, and the truth is seen much as we must suppose it to be when the spirit is disembodied. No wonder this should overpower the body. Now such cases have often stumbled those who have witnessed them and yet, so far as I have opportunity to inquire into their subsequent history, I have been persuaded that, in general, these were sound cases of conversion."

9. In the winter of 1993 the Holy Spirit addressed me and said, "If you can't jump in it, bless it. If you can't bless it, gently observe it. But if you can't patiently observe it, then just don't criticize what you don't understand!" Perhaps this is an admonition for us each to observe concerning the power and manifested presence of the Holy Spirit.

III. INCREASING IN THE ANOINTING

A. Faithfulness Issues
Luke 16:10-12 – *Whoever can be trusted with very little can also be trusted with much, and whoever is dishonest with very little will also be dishonest with much. So if you have not been trustworthy in handling worldly wealth, who will trust you with true riches? And if you have not been trustworthy with someone else's property, who will give you property of your own?*

B. Three Key Words

1. Association – Those whom you walk with will impact you.
2. Environment – An area, region or congregation can have an atmosphere of faith or unbelief, expectancy, etc.
3. Influence – What are the main things you spend your time doing? What you give your time and attention to most will greatly influence your desires and inner motivations.

C. Lessons from the "Mantle"

1. Elijah cast his mantle upon Elisha (I Kings 19:19-20).

2. Elisha catches the mantle and it covers his being
(II Kings 2:1-2; 9-10; 11-13).

3. Three practical points
   a) Acknowledge the call of God on your own life.
   b) Follow Jesus. He's the Head.
   c) Ask the Lord for "mentors".

4. We must remember the simple things!
   a) Get rest.
   b) Get filled back up.
   c) Pull away for a while.
   d) Find Him, Jesus, our Life Source.
   e) Get an outlet. Learn to laugh. Give mercy and forgiveness, and don't strike the rock.
   f) Don't take yourself too seriously

IV. SUMMATION
A testimony was given of a vision of a crystal pitcher with 92 etched on it. The words came, "We are going for the double." What is the double?

A. The Fullness of Power
The nine gifts of the Holy Spirit represent the fullness of the power of God. Ask, seek, and knock on God's door for "More Lord". (See the study guide *Releasing Spiritual Gifts* for more on this subject).

B. The Fullness of Character
The nine fruits of the Holy Spirit represent the character of Christ we desire to bear. Let us be a people of the cross of Christ and bear His character.

C. Our Goal – Gifts that Bear Fruit
Yes, our goal is to let love be our aim (character) and yet earnestly desire the spiritual gifts (Power – I Cor. 14:1).
Let us have as our goal that we are going for the double – Character that can carry the Gift and the gifts that bear fruit.

Reflection Questions
Lesson Eleven: Cooperating with the Anointing

Answers to these questions can be found in the back of the study guide.

Fill in the Blank

1. From this lesson why can you have confidence in "Calling for the Holy Spirit" _____
   _____

2. List three scripture references to the phenomena called "Falling in the Spirit". 1. _____ 2. _____ 3. _____

3. To increase the anointing in your life, what are the main things you can spend your time doing for this to increase? _____
   _____

Multiple Choice – Choose the best answer from the list below:

A.	Fullness	C.	Character
B.	Deity	D.	Faith

4. The nine fruits of the Holy Spirit represent the _____ of Christ.

5. The nine gifts of the Holy Spirit represent the _____
   of the power gifts.

True or False

6. Ask, seek, and knock on God's door for "More Lord". _____

7. Our goal is to let love be our aim and yet earnestly desire the spiritual gifts. _____

8. What you give your time and attention to most, will greatly influence your desires and inner motivations. _____

Scripture Memorization

9. Write out and memorize Luke 16:10-12.

Continued on the next page.

10. What was the primary point you learned from this lesson?

Lesson Twelve:
Moving with the Anointing

Introduction

Those whom God is using today are not being used because they are anything important. It is for one reason and one reason alone. They have touched God and God has touched them.

In July of 1983 the Lord spoke to me and said: "Five minutes of My anointed prayer through you will do more than five hours of counseling that you have done in the past." That is not saying counseling has no value. The Lord was simply presenting a principle to me. He was saying five minutes of My (His) anointing through you can affect a person's life to a greater degree that what <u>your</u> human counseling can do.

I.   THE GIFT OF PAIN

Before looking at more lessons on the anointing, let's first pause and consider the purpose of pain. Though "pain" is not technically listed in the scriptures as a spiritual gift, redemptively the feelings of pain can be used (when interpreted correctly) as a tool in the Masters hand.

A.   A Compassionate Intercessory Anointing

1. The gift of pain is where you enter into His feelings for others. Perhaps you could call it an intercessory anointing where you identify with the needs of others. (See the lesson "Identification in Intercession").

2. This pain may not leave you until that intercessory activity you have engaged in, has been discharged back to God's care.

3. At times we are called to enter into "The fellowship of Christ suffering" as in Phil. 3:10 – I want to know Christ and the power of his resurrection and the fellowship of sharing in his sufferings, becoming like him in his death.

B.   Feeling the Pain

1. A key to moving in the Spirit is when you open your heart to feel the pain or emotions of others. Do you feel the pain of others?

2. Inner vows, hardness of heart, abusive situations etc. can sear our conscious from feeling and we can end up feeling nothing. Oh that God would strip away the veils of our heart and sensitize and tenderize us to feel another's pain!

3. Do you let the eyes of the Holy Spirit look through the windows of your house (God's house)? Do you look with the eyes of your heart (spirit) into situations so you can be moved upon by God with compassion?

4. Jeremiah was called the weeping prophet. Why? Perhaps because he felt the pain of situations, circumstances, or God's heart for the people...

5. Being willing to feel another's pain is one of the keys to moving in the healing anointing of Jesus.

II. HOW DOES THE HOLY SPIRIT MOVE?

A. Three Divergent Ways of Ministering:

1. Pray by what you see in the natural that the Holy Spirit is doing. Here you are calling forth the Spirit to be released upon a person and then you are blessing what you observe the Father doing. You are then looking upon the natural effects upon a person as the Holy Spirit moves.

2. Pray by what you see with your Spiritual eyes.
    What does the Holy Spirit want to do? In this type of prayer, you may see pictures, visions, impressions, an unction, sensing, etc. You then invoke the Lords presence on what you perceive He wants to do. This is praying by spiritual insight. (Revelatory prayer)

3. Pray by Faith.
    You pray for people because the bible tells us you to it! Though you may not feel or sense anything you act in raw obedience to the Scriptures. Here we have to risk and step out.

B. Options to Moving in the Anointing
At times there appears to be options that we choose from to move in the anointing: knowing when to jump in and flow and at others times to pull back and wait on Him. In this we must learn dependency and sensitivity to the Holy Spirit.

You may minister:
1. Out of pain – fellowship from Christ's fellowship.
2. Out of a tangible or manifested presence.
3. With no feeling but having heard a word.
4. The anointing for healing.
5. From reading the scriptures and then simply doing it.
   All are effective and all have their place. The Lord may use any or all of these ways. The key to understand is this: There is no one way that is correct. You have to remain sensitive to the Holy Spirit.

C. Try on Many Shoes or Hats

Try on many different shoes or hats of the anointing as you learn to flow with Him. Eventually there will be a time in your life that you will know what you can best fit in, to employ and "serve up" to the body of Christ.

According to I Pet. 4:11–12 – Each one should use whatever gift he has received to serve others, faithfully administering God's grace in its various forms. If anyone speaks, he should do it as one speaking the very words of God. If anyone serves, he should do it with the strength God provides, so that in all things God may be praised through Jesus Christ. To Him be the glory and the power forever and ever. Amen.

You will learn which hat (special gifting) best fits you. This will be the place where the grace or anointing of the Holy Spirit will flow in the deepest manner in and through your life.

D. Wisdom Ways to Moving in the Anointing

1. The main thing to learn in the anointing is realizing it is not you. Healing Evangelist Mahesh Chavda likens the anointing to getting a scuba diving suit, a second skin, put on you. You realize it is not about you, but about Jesus Christ.
   We are to step into Him and Him into us (John 15).

2. The anointing is simple. It is a Relationship. It's asking the Holy Spirit questions: What is this? Do I say it? What now? Where from here? Ask questions, etc....

3. When the anointing seems to be lifting, humility is a key to receiving back his presence His anointing. Humble yourself before God and receive fresh grace.

4. Faithfulness is a major key to walking out the desire to see healing, deliverance and salvation take place. Be faithful in the little and more will come.

E. How Does the Anointing Increase?

1. By hanging out with those who love the anointing. Watch, observe and learn from those who know these ways of the Lord.
2. By being in the right environment – atmospheres of faith.
3. By hungering and thirsting after His presence.
4. Studying the Word and praying the promises back to the Father.
5. Persistence
6. Faithfulness etc.

III. HOW DO YOU MOVE IN THE SPIRIT

A. Three Simple Steps

1. Seek the Lord beforehand.
2. Be attentive to Him during it (meeting/engagement).
3. Risk – Step out He gives you enough to get you moving, but not enough, that there won't be an element of risk, so as to keep you always looking to Him.

IV. KEYS TO THE ANOINTING

A. The Jealousy of God
Understand the jealousy of God and the fear of the Lord. Realizing it is Him and not you who is at work. He is a "Jealous God" and will not share His glory with another.

B. Thank Offerings
Author and teacher Bob Mumford once said: "I give the trophies I have received during the course of a day back to the Lord at the end of the day and worship Him with them." Thanksgiving is the track that carries the mighty payload of faith!

C. Stepping Out of the Way
He doesn't always need you. You are not there to perform. Avoid the "messiah complex" that everything revolves around you. Step out of the way and let Him move in His unique manner.

D. Patience
This is the virtue that none of us wants, but all of us needs. Martin Luther, the great Protestant reformationist said – "He starved out the devil by patience."

E. **Worship and Praise**
This is a place before Him. He is enthroned upon the praise of His people (Psa. 22:3). Where He is, His life will emanate from.

F. **Stop and Admit Failure**
Let's pause and wait on the Lord for perhaps we missed Him. Be willing to humble yourself; retrace your steps; and pick back up where He left off!

G. **Fasting**
Charles Finney, the great 19th century revivalist would go into times of fasting when he felt the manifested presence subside. He would fast to call forth the tangible anointing. We can do the same.

H. **Voice of Holy Spirit**
Practice the habit to listening to His still small voice. The more you practice, the better you'll hear. (See the study guide – *Prophetic Foundations*, Lesson Five: "Practical Suggestions on Hearing God's Voice" for more on this subject.)

I. **Thunder! Fire!**
Call forth the demonstrative impact of His overpowering presence! Watch out! He might not appear as the Gentle Shepherd, but the Lion of Judah who roars.

J. **Strategic Times**
Realize in certain circumstances, He has a specific timing He wants to release His activity.

K. **Compassion**
Ask the Lord for a revelation of mercy, brokenness and compassion of the Lord. (See Lesson Nine: "Compassion – A Necessary Ingredient" in this study guide for more on this subject).

L. **Faith**
There is no substitute for faith. We must step out and make room for God! Remember faith is spelt - R-I-S-K.

V. **NEGATIVE RESPONSES TO THE HOLY SPIRIT**
We are not just to be open to the Holy Spirit, but we are to passionately pursue Him (I Cor. 14:1). But there are several warnings given to us in scriptures of attitudes and actions to avoid in our relationship with and to the Holy Spirit.

A. **Do Not Neglect or Ignorant**
Paul uses the word ignorant thirteen times in the epistles.

I Cor.12:1 – *Now about spiritual gifts, brothers, I do not want you to be ignorant.* (NIV)

B. Do Not Tempt

Acts 5:9 – *Peter said to her, "How could you agree to test the Spirit of the Lord? Look! The feet of the men who buried your husband are at the door, and they will carry you out also."*

C. Do Not Grieve

Eph. 4:29-31 – *Do not let any unwholesome talk come out of your mouths, but only what is helpful for building others up according to their needs, that it may benefit those who listen. And do not grieve the Holy Spirit of God, with whom you were sealed for the day of redemption. Get rid of all bitterness, rage and anger, brawling and slander, along with every form of malice.*

D. Do Not Quench

I Thess. 5:19 – *Do not put out the Spirit's fire.*

E. Do Not Insult

Heb. 10:29 – *How much more severely do you think a man deserves to be punished who has trampled the Son of God under foot, who has treated as an unholy thing the blood of the covenant that sanctified him, and who has insulted the Spirit of grace?* When you insult someone, they remove their presence from you.

F. Do Not Blaspheme

Matt. 12:31-33 – *And so I tell you, every sin and blasphemy will be forgiven men, but the blasphemy against the Spirit will not be forgiven. Anyone who speaks a word against the Son of Man will be forgiven, but anyone who speaks against the Holy Spirit will not be forgiven, either in this age or in the age to come. "Make a tree good and its fruit will be good, or make a tree bad and its fruit will be bad, for a tree is recognized by its fruit.*

VI. THREE THINGS TO ALWAYS DO WITH THE HOLY SPIRIT

A. Honor Him Always As Your Guest

Welcome Him on a first-name basis without over familiarity. Acknowledge Him as the third person of the Godhead, with His own distinct personality (John 16:13). Honor Him and desire His presence. Mahesh Chavda said: "The more I walk with Him, the more gentle His voice is becomes. Open up your heart, your most intimate place, and honor the third person of the Godhead."

B. Seek Him

Ask for Him and seek to be equipped by Him (Luke 7:7-11). He is more than "special guest". He is our equipper. Ask the Father in Jesus' name to be equipped by the Holy Spirit to do the ministry work.

C. Give Him Freedom and Liberty

Yield to Him (II Cor. 3:17). When the Holy Spirit is Lord, there will be freedom for the people. Let the Holy Spirit be in control.

VII. FIVE PRINCIPLES OF HOW THE HOLY SPIRIT ALWAYS MOVES

Read John 14:16-21 and John 16:5-15 before proceeding into the following points.

A. In and Through (by means of) the Written Scriptures

He never moves contrary to the Word of God. He compliments and does not compete with the Word of God.

B. In Agreement with the Father and the Son

There are never three wills in the Godhead. The Holy Spirit reveals the council of the Father and the Son.

C. Brings Jesus into a Greater Reality

The Holy Spirit reveals Jesus as a living reality, and brings us into a deeper relationship with Him.

D. A Life-Giving Source

He brings us into the life of the Lord Jesus. He is interested in maturing our character, not just bringing us personal comfort.
He is interested in bringing us truth, not false assurance or consolation. He woos, convicts, shepherds, and leads us to the life-source of God.

E. Moving the Believer to Be a Witness

He helps us overcome our fears and He stretches us outside of ourselves, bringing both maturity and fruit. He motivates us to testify of the love and power of God.

VIII. PREPARATIONS TO FLOW IN THE HOLY SPIRIT

A. Avoid Hurrying or Rushing

Quiet yourself before the Lord, Avoid being like a stirred-up fish bowl and rest before His presence.
Psa. 130:5-6 – *I wait for the Lord, my soul waits, and in his word I put my hope. My soul waits for the Lord more than watchmen wait for the morning, more than watchmen wait for the morning* (NIV).

Psa. 131:2 – *But I have stilled and quieted my soul; like a weaned child with its mother, like a weaned child is my soul within me.*

B. Pray in the Spirit

Build yourself up, in your faith by praying in the gift of tongues. This will edify your faith and turn you into the Fathers heart. I Cor. 14:4.

C. Get Involved

Seek God for something to take when you attend a gathering. Purpose in your heart to get involved and don't go just to receive.

D. God Wants to Use You!

Yes! God wants to use little ole me! Believe that the Lord wants to use me to impart to others.

E. It's Only by GRACE!

Ask God for a revelation of Grace. That way all the glory goes to God to whom it all belongs.

Remember you earn your wings every day.

Reflection Questions
Lesson Twelve: Moving with the Anointing

Answers to these questions can be found in the back of the study guide.

Fill in the Blank

1. The main thing to learn in the anointing is realizing it is not _____.
2. List five things to increase the anointing in your life! 1. _____
   2. _____ 3. _____
   4. _____ 5. _____
3. The gift of pain is where you enter into His feelings for _____.

Multiple Choice – Choose the best answer from the list below:

A.	Categories	C.	Pain
B.	Options	D.	Joy

4. Being willing to feel another's _____ is one of the keys to moving in the healing anointing of Jesus.
5. At times there appears to be _____ that we choose from to move in the anointing.

True or False

6. This pain may not leave you until that intercessory activity you have engaged in, has been discharged back to God's care. _____
7. A key to moving in the Spirit is when you open your heart to feel the pain or emotions of others. _____
8. Inner vows, hardness of heart and abusive situations can sear our conscious from feeling and we can end up feeling nothing. _____

Scripture Memorization

9. Write out and memorize Philippians 3:10 and I Peter 4:11.

Continued on the next page.

10. What was the primary point you learned from this lesson?

Answers to the Reflection Questions

Lesson One: The Healing Ministry of Jesus
1. Atonement – Refer to this lesson.
2. Sozo – Refer to this lesson.
3. Repentance
4. Signs
5. Signs
6.   True   7. True   8. True

Lesson Two: Healing Delivery Systems
1. Communion; Water Baptism; Calling for the Elders and Anointing with Oil ; Laying on of Hands and Prayer by Believers; By the Spoken Word; Jesus' Garments; Peter's Shadow; Handkerchiefs and Aprons from Paul; Levels of the Operation; Confession; Healing Release through Angelic Activity.
2. 1. The natural   2. Science and the medical arts   3. Divine, supernatural healing.
3. Healing, cleansing and restoration
4. Jesus Christ
5.   True   6. True   7. True

Lesson Three: Five Stage Healing Model
1. The Interview, Diagnostic decision, Prayer selection, Prayer engagement, Post prayer decision.
2. Prayer directed toward God and Prayer from God.
3. Supernatural
4. Misdiagnosis
5.   False   6. False   7. True

Lesson Four: Using a Word of Knowledge in Healing
1 Refer to the definitions of David Pytches, Peter Wagner and Derek Prince in this lesson.
2. This could come in the form of dreams, impressions, spontaneous prophecy, spiritual sight etc.
3. Difficulty lies with the person receiving ministry or giving ministry. The Holy Spirit becomes offended and withdraws. The enemy resists God's plan.
4. Obstacles
5. Worship
6.   True   7. True   8. False

Lesson Five: God's Remedy for Rejection
1. Express your own thoughts.
2. Express your own thoughts.
3. Feeling
4. Acceptance
5.   True   6. True   7. False

Lesson Six – Healing the Wounded Spirit
1. Proverbs 18:14
2. Proverbs 4:10
3. Hurtful
4. Introverted
5. Forgiveness
6.   True   7. True   8. False

Lesson Seven - Breaking Emotional Bondages
1. Refer to I A, B, C – A Definition of Terms.
2. Refer to I D
3. Memories
4. Offense
5.   True   6. True   7. True

Lesson Eight – Transformation of the Mind
1. Personal answer.
2. Hope
3. Good
4.   True   5. False   6. True

Lesson Nine – Compassion – A Necessary Ingredient
1. SPLANCHNIZOMAI: to be moved as to one's inwards, to be moved with compassion, to yearn with compassion, is frequently recorded of Christ towards the multitude and towards individual sufferers – Matt. 9:6 2.
2. OIKTERO: to have pity, a feeling of distress through the ills of others, is used of God's compassion Rom. 9:15.
3. SUMPATHEO: to suffer with another, to be affected similarly (Eng., sympathy), to have compassion upon, Heb. 10:34, of compassion for those in prison, is translated "be touched with" in Hebrews 4:15, of Christ as the High Priest.
4. Eruption
5. Identify
6.   True   7. False   8. False

Lesson Ten – Understanding the Anointing
1. In Hebrew – "anointing" and "Messiah" come from the same root.
The Greek word for Christ, *Cristos*, means "the anointed one". The anointing is the person of Jesus Christ manifesting Himself by grace. It can be both a residential grace gift of the Holy Spirit given from God now within the person or it can be a circumstantial gifting occasionally coming upon a person.
2. Yoke defined – Heavy, oppressing, burden that weighs you down.
Something that is put upon you (sometimes to join you with another) for the purpose of channeling you into usefulness.
3. Anointing
4. Teaches
5.   True   6. True   7. True

Lesson Eleven – Cooperating with the Anointing
1. The Scriptures teach us that we can ask for the Holy Spirit.
Church growth in Acts was triggered with a manifestation of God's power through signs and wonders.
The anointing of power through the Holy Spirit accomplishes the "release" of the gifts of the Spirit and allows God to initiate spiritual ministry.
Experientially, it releases blessing, anointing, and ministry.
2. Ezek. 1:28; Dan 10:9; Rev. 1:17
3. Personal Answer – Eg. Bible Reading, Prayer, Hanging around those who carry the anointing etc
4. Character
5. Fullness
6.   True   7. True   8. True

Lesson Twelve – Moving with the Anointing

1. You
2. By hanging out with those who love the anointing. Watch, observe and learn from those who know these ways of the Lord; By being in the right environment/atmospheres of faith; By hungering and thirsting after His presence; Persistence; Faithfulness; Studying the Word and praying the promises back to the Father.
3. Others
4. Pain
5. Options
6. True   7. True   8. True

Resource Materials

Ken Blue, *Authority to Heal*, InterVarsity Press, Downers Grove, IL, 1987.

Michael Brown. *Israel's Divine Healer*, Zondervan, Grand Rapids, MI, 1995.

Rodney Howard-Browne, *The Touch of God*, Louisville: R.H.B.E.A. Publications, 1992.

F. F. Bosworth, *Christ the Healer*, Fleming Revell, Grand Rapids, MI, 1973.

Mahesh Chavda, *Only Love Can Make a Miracle*, Ann Arbor: Servant Publications, 1990.

A. J. Gordon, *The Ministry of Healing*, Harrisburg Christian Publ.,1882.

Kenneth Hagin, *Understanding the Anointing*, Tulsa, OK: Kenneth Hagin Ministries, pp. 163-165.

Charles and Frances Hunter, *To Heal the Sick*, Kingwood: Hunter Books, 1983.

Hugh Jeter, *By His Stripes*, Gospel Publishing House, Springfield, MO, 1977.

Francis MacNutt, *Healing*, Notre Dame: Ave Maria Press, 1974.

Francis MacNutt, *Overcome by the Spirit*, Old Tappen: Fleming H. Revel, 1990.

Francis MacNutt, *The Power to Heal*, Notre Dame: Ave Maria Press, 1985.

Watchman Nee, *Spiritual Authority*, New York: Christian Fellowship Publishers, Inc., 1972.

T. L. Osborn, *Healing the Sick*, Tulsa: Harrison House, 1959.

George Otis, *Like a Roaring Lion*, Van Nuys: Time-Light Publishers, 1973.

Derek Prince, "From Rejection to Acceptance" (Booklet).

Derek Prince, *Spiritual Warfare*, Springdale: Whitaker House, 1987, Derek Prince Publications, 1971.

Derek Prince, "The Nine Gifts of the Holy Spirit" (Tape set), Ft. Lauderdale, FL:

David Pytches, *Spiritual Gifts in the Local Church*, Minneapolis, MN: Bethany House Publishers, 1971.

John and Mark Sandford, *Deliverance and Inner Healing*, Chosen, books, Grand Rapids, MI, 1992.

John and Paula Sandford, *Transforming the Inner Man: God's Powerful Principles for Inner Healing and Lasting Life Change*, Charisma House, 2007.

David A. Seamands, *Healing of Memories*, Wheaton: Victor Books, 1985.

Dean Sherman, *Spiritual Warfare for Every Christian: How to Live in Victory and Retake the Land*, Seattle: YWAM Publishing, 1990.

A. B. Simpson, *The Gospel of Healing*, Christian Alliance Publishers., New York, NY, 1915.

Betty Tapscott, *Inner Healing through Healing of Memories*, Houston, TX: Tapscott Ministries, 1984.

Vine's Expository Dictionary for New Testament Words.

C. Peter Wagner, *Territorial Spirits: Insights on Strategic-Level Spiritual Warfare from Nineteen Christian Leaders*, Chichester: Sovereign World Ltd., 1991.

C. Peter Wagner and F. Douglas Pennoyer, *Wrestling with Dark Angels*, Ventura, CA: Regal Books, 1990.

C. Peter Wagner, *Your Spiritual Gifts*, Ventura, CA: Regal Books, 1994.

Webster's Dictionary

Thomas B. White, *The Believer's Guide to Spiritual Warfare*, Ann Arbor: Servant Publications, 1990.

John Wimber with Kevin Springer, *Power Healing*, San Francisco: Harper and Row, Publishers, 1987.

John Wimber, "Signs and Wonders Syllabus", MC 511, Anaheim, CA: Vineyard Ministries International, 1985.

.

End Notes

1   A. J. Gordon, *The Ministry of Healing*, Harrisburg Christian Publ.,1882, pp. 16-17.

2   A. B. Simpson, *The Gospel of Healing*, New York, NY: Christian Alliance, 1915, pp.15-17.

3   F. F. Bosworth, *Christ the Healer*, Grand Rapids, MI: Fleming Revell, 1973 (1877) pp.40.

4   T. L. Osborn, *Healing the Sick*, Tulsa, OK: OSFO Foundation, 1959, pp. 151

5   Hugh Jeter, *By His Stripes*, Springfield, MO: Gospel Publishing House, 1977, pp. 34-35.

6   John Wimber and Kevin Springer, *Power Healing*, Harper, San Francisco CA, 1987, pp. 35.

7   Ibid., p. 61.

8   John and Mark Sanford, *Deliverance and Inner Healing*, Grand Rapids, MI: Chosen, Books, 1992, pp. 50.

9   Michael Brown. *Israel's Divine Healer*, Grand Rapids, MI: Zondervan, 1995, pp. 28-36.

10   John Wimber and Kevin Springer, *Power Healing*, San Francisco, CA: Harper, 1987, pp. 245.

11   Ibid., pp. 198-235.

12   David Pytches, *Spiritual Gifts in the Local Church*, Minneapolis, MN: Bethany, 1971.

13   C. Peter Wagner, Your Spiritual Gifts, Ventura: Regal, 1994.

14   Derek Prince, "The Nine Gifts of the Holy Spirit" (Tape Series), Ft. Lauderdale, FL: Derek Prince, 1971.

15   This material has come from the wonderful teaching influence of Derek Prince's ministry and from personal life experiences of James W. Goll. For more on this subject see the teaching tape and booklet by Derek Prince "From Rejection to Acceptance".

16   John Wimber, "Signs and Wonders Syllabus," MC511, Anaheim: Vineyard Ministries Int'l., 1985.

17   John and Paula Sandford, *Transforming the Inner Man: God's Powerful Principles for Inner Healing and Lasting Life Change*, Charisma House, 2007.

18   Op. cit., Signs and Wonders Syllabus MC 511.

19   Op. cit., Signs and Wonders Syllabus MC 511.

20   Op. cit., Signs and Wonders Syllabus MC 511.

21   David Seamands, *Healing of Memories*, Wheaton: Victor, 1985.

22   Op. cit., Signs and Wonders Syllabus MC 511.

23   Betty Tapscott, *Inner Healing through Healing of Memories*, Houston: Tapscott Ministries, 1984.

24   Op cit., Signs and Wonders Syllabus MC 511,

25   Op cit., Signs and Wonders Syllabus MC 511,

26   Webster's Collegiate Dictionary, 10th Edition, Springfield, MA: Merriam-Webster, Inc., 1994), 234.

27 W. E. Vine, Vine's Expository Dictionary of New Testament Words, Nashville: Thomas Nelson Publishers, 1985.

28 Ken Blue, *The Authority to Heal*, Downers Grove: Varsity, 1987.

29 Op cit., John Wimber and Kevin Springer, *Power Healing*, pp. 47-48.

30 Ibid., pp. 52-54.

31 Mahesh Chavda, *Only Love Makes a Miracle*, pp. 72-73.

32 Ibid, pp. 74-77.

33 Rodney Howard-Browne, *The Touch of God*, Louisville: RHBEA., 1992.

34 Kenneth Hagin, *Understanding the Anointing*, Tulsa, OK: Kenneth Hagin Ministries, pp. 163-165.

35 David Pytches, *Spiritual Gifts in the Local Church*, Minneapolis, MN: Bethany House Publishers, 1971.

36 Ibid., David Pytches.

37 Francis MacNutt, *Overcome by the Spirit*, Old Tappan: Fleming H. Revell, 1990, pages 88-89.

38 Ibid., pp. 54-55.

39 Ibid., p. 58.

40 Ibid., p. 90.

41. Ibid., p. 98.

42 Ibid., pp. 99-100.

43 Ibid., pp. 104-105.

44 Ibid., pp. 110-111.

Resources

Encounters Network ~ changing lives ❖ impacting nations
P.O. Box 1653, Franklin, TN 37065
www.encountersnetwork.com | 1-877-200-1604

Encounters Network

Network Sponsorship

We need a host of people and churches who will arise and say, "We believe in God's call on E[N] and we will back you financially!"

Sponsorship Levels:

Benefits:

Foundation Sponsor

Any amount given monthy or a one time gift of $250-$999 per year

20% off EN Conference registration
15% off EN Bookstore through website and call center
Reserved seating at EN Conferences
Quarterly EN Update Packet
One Time Free Gift

Executive Sponsor

$100-$499 per month or a one time gift of $1,000-$4,999 per year

Foundation Sponsor Benefits PLUS
50% off EN Conference registration
20% off EN Bookstore through website and call center

Presidential Sponsor

$500 or more per month or a one time gift of $5,000 or more per year

Executive Sponsor Benefits PLUS
2 Free EN Conference registrations, registration is required
25% off EN Bookstore through website and call center

For more information please call 1-877-200-1604 or
visit our website at www.encountersnetwork.com

COMPASSION ACTS
love taking action

Love Taking Action

◆ Mission Projects
sending resources and volunteers to help meet specific needs

◆ Rice Shipments
shipping fortified rice to fight hunger around the world

◆ Emergency Relief
responding to natural disasters through food and humanitarian aid

◆ Project Dreamers Park
buidling playgrounds and community centers to inspire children to dream

◆ First Nations in America
serving Native Americans by providing food, health supplies and education

Compassion Acts is a network of synergistic relationships between people, ministries and organizations, focused on bringing hope for our day through the power of compassion and prayer. We desire to demonstrate love and encourage the hearts of those impacted by poverty, disease, political strife and natural disasters through human relief efforts.

www.compassionacts.com

PrayerStorm

The Hour that Changes the World

Leviticus 6:13
"Fire must be kept burning on the altar continually; it must not got out."

Worldwide 24/7
Hourly Intercession Targeting:

◆ Revival in the Church
◆ Prayer for Israel
◆ World's Greatest Youth Awakening
◆ Crisis Intervention through Intercession

The vision of PrayerStorm is to restore and release the Moravian model of the watch of the Lord into churches, homes and prayer rooms around the world. Web-based teaching, prayer bulletins and resources are utilized to facilitate round-the-clock worship and prayer to win for the Lamb the rewards of His suffering.

Releasing the Global Moravian Lampstand

www.prayerstorm.com

Encounters Network
changing lives ❖ impacting nations

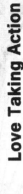

Changing Lives ❖ Impacting Nations

◆ Empowering Believers
through training and resources

◆ EN Media
relevant messages for our day

◆ God Encounters Training
e-school of the heart

◆ EN Alliance
a coalition of leaders

The vision of **Encounters Network** is to unite and mobilize the body of Christ by teaching and imparting the power of intercession and prophetic ministry, while cultivating God's heart for Israel. We accomplish this through networking with leaders in the church and marketplace; equipping believers through conferences and classes, utilizing various forms of relevant media; and creating quality materials to reproduce life in the Spirit.

www.encountersnetwork.com

Introduction to God Encounters Training School

If you are seeking to grow in your intimacy with God and mature in your walk of faith, if you desire to cultivate the spirit of revelation and live a life of power in the Spirit, then begin your journey by joining God Encounters Training – eSchool of the Heart.

Biblically-based study materials in both physical and electronic formats, combined with Spirit-led teaching, are now yours to experience on a personal level. These correspondence courses may be taken for credit towards graduation from the God Encounters Training School.

What Others Are Saying:

Goll's extraordinary ability to think through crucial issues and his skill at expressing the solutions in terms that the average believer can understand, comes through loud and clear in his materials.

~ **C. Peter Wagner**, noted author, professor, President of Global Harvest Ministries, Chancellor Emeritus of the Wagner Leadership Institute

The Lord has given James Goll insights into Scripture as it relates to the foundation of each believer and vision for the Body of Christ. His curriculum will powerfully strengthen the spiritual life of any person, group, or congregation that will use them.

~ **Don Finto**, author, pastor emeritus of Belmont Church in Nashville, TN and director of the Caleb Company

 For Course Information and Registration Visit
www.GETeSchool.com

GET eSchool Courses
& Corresponding Study Guides

CHAMBER OF ACTION
EXPLORING PRINCIPLES - EXPERIENCING POWER

DELIVERANCE FROM DARKNESS

You shall know the truth and the truth shall set you free! Through this accessible and easy-to-use guide, you will learn how to: recognize demonic entities and their strategies, equip yourself to overcome the demonic, keep yourself refreshed during the fight, bring healing through blessing, and much more!

THE HEALING ANOINTING

In this thorough study guide, James W. Goll covers a range of topics including: The Healing Ministry of Jesus, How to Move In and Cooperate with the Anointing, Healing the Wounded Spirit, Overcoming Rejection, the Five Stage Healing Model, and much more.

RELEASING SPIRITUAL GIFTS

In this study guide, James draws from scripture and adds perspective from many diverse streams to bring you clear definitions and exhort you into activation and release. The topics covered are subjects like: How Does the Holy Spirit Move, What Offends the Holy Spirit, and many other lessons from years of experience.

REVIVAL BREAKTHROUGH

James W. Goll brings 12 solid teachings on topics like: Prophetic Prayers for Revival, Classic Characteristics of Revival, Fasting Releases God's Presence, Creating an Opening, Gatekeepers of His Presence, and much more. This manual will inspire you to believe for a breakthrough in your life, neighborhood, region, city and nation for Jesus' sake!

WAR IN THE HEAVENLIES

These carefully prepared 12 detailed lessons on spiritual warfare cover topics like: The Fall of Lucifer, Dealing with Territorial Spirits, The Weapons of Our Warfare, High Praises, The Blood Sprinkled Seven Times, and other great messages. This is one of James' most thorough and complete manuals.

CHAMBER OF LIFE
BUILDING OUR FOUNDATION - KNOWING TRUTHS, GROWING IN FAITH

A RADICAL FAITH

Whether you are a veteran spiritual warrior or new believer, this accessible, comprehensive guide lays out the enduring biblical fundamentals that establish the bedrock of belief for every mature Christian. This handbook will help you build an indestructible foundation of radical faith.

DISCOVERING THE NATURE OF GOD

These lessons focus on the knowledge of God Himself. Lessons include: Laying a Proper Foundation, The Authority of God's Word, The Effects of God's Word, God as Our Father, The Nature of God, The Attributes of God, Jesus the Messiah, and more. Learn the nature of God and thus be transformed into His image.

WALKING IN THE SUPERNATURAL LIFE

James W. Goll weds together a depth of the Word with a flow of the Spirit that will ground and challenge you to live in the fullness for which God has created you. Topics include The God Who Never Changes, Tools for the Tool Belt, Finishing Well, and much more.

TO PURCHASE THESE STUDY GUIDES INDIVIDUALLY
& OTHER RELATED PRODUCT VISIT: WWW.ENCOUNTERSNETWORK.COM

For Course Information and Registration Visit
www.GETeSchool.com

GET eSchool Courses & Corresponding Study Guides

CHAMBER OF INTIMACY
BLUEPRINTS FOR PRAYER - PRELUDE TO REVIVAL

WATCHMEN ON THE WALLS

This original study guide is a classic in today's global prayer movement and covers many important and foundational lessons on intercession including: Fire on the Altar, Christ Our Priestly Model, The Watch of the Lord, From Prayer to His Presence, Identification in Intercession, and more.

COMPASSIONATE PROPHETIC INTERCESSION

These 12 lessons feature James W. Goll's finest teaching on the fundamentals of prophetic intercession and represent one of the primary messages of his life. Topics include Travail, Tears in the Bottle, Prophetic Intercession, The Power of Proclamation, Praying in the Spirit, and much more.

PRAYER STORM

This study guide sounds a worldwide call to consistent, persistent prayer for: revival in the church, the greatest youth awakening ever, Israel – and for all the descendents of Abraham, and God's intervention in times of major crises. Prayer Storm is an invitation into an international virtual house of prayer full of intercessors who commit to pray one hour per week.

PRAYERS OF THE NEW TESTAMENT

In this study guide, James goes through each of the scriptural prayers of the early church apostles and brings you a brief historical background sketch along with insights from the Holy Spirit for today. Learn what true apostolic intercession is, how to intercede with revelation, and how to cultivate a heart for your city and nation.

STRATEGIES OF INTERCESSION

In these 12 lessons, James W. Goll deals with issues like Confessing Generational Sins, Reminding God of His Word, Praying for Those in Authority, Praying on Site with Insight, and Praying Your Family into God's Family. It is a thorough and precise exposure to the many different strategies and models of prayer.

CONSECRATED CONTEMPLATIVE PRAYER

These 12 lessons have helped hundreds come into a deeper communion with their heavenly Father. James W. Goll brings understanding from the truths of Christian mystics of the past and builds on it with lessons from his own walk with the Lord. Topics include The Ministry of Fasting, Contemplative Prayer, Quieting Our Souls before God, and much more.

TO PURCHASE THESE STUDY GUIDES INDIVIDUALLY & OTHER RELATED PRODUCT VISIT: WWW.ENCOUNTERSNETWORK.COM

For Course Information and Registration Visit
www.GETeSchool.com

PROPHETIC FOUNDATIONS

Does God really speak to us personally today? If I listen, will I understand what He says? For those desiring to hear God, this course will show how anyone can both listen and speak to God. Lessons include: A Biblical History of the Prophetic, Intimacy in the Prophetic, Seven Expressions of the Prophetic, The Prophetic Song of the Lord, Responding to Revelation, and more.

MATURATION IN THE PROPHETIC

You can grow in the things of the prophetic! These 12 lessons include: The Calling, Training and Commissioning; The Cross: The Prophetic Lifestyle; Pits and Pinnacles of the Prophetic; The Seer and the Prophet; Women in the Prophetic; and more. Character issues and relational dynamics are discussed at length.

RECEIVING AND DISCERNING REVELATION

This study guide will introduce you to the ways of God and the Spirit of Revelation and how to discern what is from the Holy Spirit and what is not. Learn to grow in your capacity to receive revelatory things from the Holy Spirit, and discern the voice and ways of God with nine scriptural tests to judging revelation.

DISCOVERING THE SEER IN YOU

What is the difference between a Seer and a Prophet? How do you cultivate the revelatory presence of the Lord? Is there a key that authentically opens the heavens? This guide helps you find and release the special gifts God has given to you, reveals how you can cultivate this realm of the prophetic in your life, and grounds you in the Word of God concerning prophetic gifts, dreams, visions, and open heavens.

EXPLORING THE NATURE AND GIFT OF DREAMS

This insightful study guide equips you for a greater understanding of the language of dreams, and grounds you in the Word of God concerning dreams and how to interpret them. This key to unlocking your gift of dreams explores: Cultivating a Culture for Revelation, Dream Drainers, Dream Busters, Why God Seems Silent and How to Cultivate the Realm of the Prophetic in your life.

UNDERSTANDING SUPERNATURAL ENCOUNTERS

This in-depth study guide contains 12 lessons that will give you insight on subjects like: Prophetic Gestures and Actions, Keys to the Supernatural, The Deception of the Anointing, Trances, Levels of Supernatural Visions, Order and Characteristics of Angels, Ministry and Function of Angels, and much more!

ANGELIC ENCOUNTERS

James and Michal Ann Goll use Scripture, church history, testimonies, and personal experience to: describe the different categories of angels, explain angels' ministry as God's agents to the world, demonstrate how intercession and angelic ministry are related, and show you how to perceive and engage angels in your own life.

For Course Information and Registration Visit
www.GETeSchool.com

Made in the USA
Charleston, SC
08 September 2012